MANAGEMENT INFORMATION SYSTEMS

INDRAJIT CHATTERJEE
Professor and Vice Principal
IIAS School of Management
Siliguri Campus

PHI Learning Private Limited
New Delhi-110001
2010

Rs. 195.00

MANAGEMENT INFORMATION SYSTEMS
Indrajit Chatterjee

© 2010 by PHI Learning Private Limited, New Delhi. All rights reserved. No part of this book may be reproduced in any form, by mimeograph or any other means, without permission in writing from the publisher.

ISBN-978-81-203-4023-7

The export rights of this book are vested solely with the publisher.

Published by Asoke K. Ghosh, PHI Learning Private Limited, M-97, Connaught Circus, New Delhi-110001 and Printed by Mudrak, 30-A, Patparganj, Delhi-110091.

*Dedicated to
Koel Chatterjee, a woman entrepreneur*

Dedicated to
Rod Chapman, a known anonymym

Contents

Preface   *ix*

Chapter 1   **INTRODUCTION**   **1–10**

    1.1   Information Management   *1*
    1.2   Business Perspective   *5*
    1.3   Technology   *7*
    1.4   Management Process—Planning of Information System   *8*
    Review Questions   *9*
    Discussion Questions   *10*

Chapter 2   **MANAGEMENT INFORMATION SYSTEMS (MIS)**   **11–20**

    2.1   Definition and Need   *11*
    2.2   Resource Requirements of Management Information Systems (MIS)   *12*
    2.3   Major Types of Systems in the Organization   *13*
    2.4   Development of Management Information Systems (MIS)   *17*
    2.5   Implementation of Management Information Systems (MIS)   *19*
    Review Questions   *19*
    Discussion Questions   *20*

Chapter 3   **HARDWARE**   **21–32**

    3.1   Computer Architecture   *21*
    3.2   Processing Unit   *23*
    3.3   Storage   *23*
    3.4   Computer Types   *26*
    3.5   Input/Output Devices   *27*
    Review Questions   *31*
    Discussion Questions   *32*

Chapter 4   SOFTWARE   33–42

    4.1   Operating System and System Software   *33*
    4.2   Multiprogramming, Multiprocessing and Time Sharing   *34*
    4.3   Programming Language and Utility Software   *37*
    4.4   End-user and Office Automation   *39*

Review Questions   41
Discussion Questions   42

Chapter 5   DATABASE MANAGEMENT   43–54

    5.1   File Organization   *43*
    5.2   Database Management   *46*
    5.3   Database Design   *47*
    5.4   Management and Database   *51*

Review Questions   54
Discussion Questions   54

Chapter 6   BUSINESS DATA COMMUNICATION   55–69

    6.1   Data Communication and Network   *55*
    6.2   Communication Media   *56*
    6.3   Network Topology   *62*
    6.4   Network Classifications   *64*

Review Questions   69
Discussion Questions   69

Chapter 7   APPLICATION OF INFORMATION SYSTEMS   70–86

    7.1   Application in Manufacturing Sector   *70*
    7.2   Marketing Information System   *71*
    7.3   Financial Information System   *72*
    7.4   Production Information System   *74*
    7.5   Human Resource Information System   *75*
    7.6   Business Process Outsourcing (BPO)   *77*

Review Questions   86
Discussion Questions   86

Chapter 8   ORGANIZATION AND INFORMATION SYSTEM   87–93

    8.1   Relationship between Organization and Information System   *87*
    8.2   Effects of Organization on Information System   *89*
    8.3   Impact of Information Technology on Organization Design   *91*

Review Questions   93
Discussion Questions   93

Chapter 9 SYSTEM ANALYSIS AND DESIGN   94–106

9.1 Introduction to Information System Development *94*
9.2 System Development Methodologies *96*
9.3 Managing System Development Process *104*

Review Questions 105
Discussion Questions 106

Chapter 10 E-COMMERCE   107–120

10.1 Foundation of Electronic Commerce *107*
10.2 Retailing *110*
10.3 Service Industry *113*
10.4 Market Research *117*
10.5 Electronic Commerce Strategy and Implementation *118*

Review Questions 120
Discussion Questions 120

Chapter 11 SUPPLY CHAIN MANAGEMENT   121–128

11.1 Competitive Advantage of Supply Chain Management *121*
11.2 Managing Supply Chain Management *123*
11.3 Supply Chain: Value Engineering *125*

Review Questions 127
Discussion Questions 128

Chapter 12 CUSTOMER RELATIONSHIP MANAGEMENT (CRM) 129–141

12.1 Customer Relationship Management—A Framework *129*
12.2 Customer Relationship Management (CRM) *132*
12.3 Customer Value Management *134*
12.4 Customer Relationship Management and Data Management *137*

Review Questions 141
Discussion Questions 141

Chapter 13 DECISION SUPPORT SYSTEMS   142–156

13.1 Introduction *142*
13.2 Communication Driven Decision Support System *145*
13.3 Data Driven Decision Support System *146*
13.4 Document Driven Decision Support System *147*
13.5 Model Driven Decision Support System *149*
13.6 Trend in Decision Support System *153*

Review Questions 156
Discussion Questions 156

Chapter 14   EXECUTIVE INFORMATION SYSTEM   157–163

14.1 Introduction   *157*
14.2 Executive Information Needs   *159*
14.3 Computer-based Executive Information System   *160*
14.4 Management Challenges   *162*

Review Questions   163
Discussion Questions   164

Chapter 15   KNOWLEDGE MANAGEMENT   165–173

15.1 Introduction   *165*
15.2 Managing Knowledge and Knowledge Workers   *167*
15.3 Knowledge Management in Electronic Business   *170*

Review Questions   172
Discussion Questions   172

Chapter 16   INFORMATION SYSTEMS: ETHICAL AND SOCIAL ISSUES   174–179

16.1 Ethical and Social Issues   *174*
16.2 Ethics and Moral Dimensions   *176*
16.3 Management Challenges   *177*

Review Questions   179
Discussion Questions   179

Appendix I   CASE STUDIES   181–193

Hotel is Hot   181
Software is Soft   183
Organization: Can You Organize?   185
Supply Chain Management—A Pharmaceutical Company   188
Close Down or Not to Close Down   191

Glossary   195–196

References   197–198

Index   199–202

Preface

In today's age of information, Management Information Systems, i.e. MIS has become a vital tool for decision making. The use of computers has spread across all the functional areas in any organization. The computer has become a driving force in all sorts of activities in business. It helps in modern scientific investigation and engineering problem solving. Hence it is imperative that all executives across the organization acquire knowledge in the area of information technology.

Information system management has made a major impact in organizational development. Competition has taken a new direction in business environment. The word "competitive advantage" has changed its definition in the era of globalization. At the same time, information is readily available to consumers and they are empowered much more than yesteryears. As a result, a sea change has been taking place throughout organizations. This has given birth to new ways of managing information.

Electronic commerce is generating new business models through internet. The repository nature of the data in the internet holds a huge potential for the development of information management. A new society has evolved as internet society. As a result, new areas have emerged like customer relationship management, supply chain management, knowledge management, etc. It ultimately leads to new developments in the area of information technology as well as information management. Data mining is another area in knowledge management.

This book reflects major areas in information systems with contemporary issues and their effect on business and organization. Some fundamental areas are also covered for general readers.

In the course of my teaching, specially Business Management and my industrial experience in the area of information management, I started to develop study material for classroom discussions. Over the years, I decided to develop a book on Management Information Systems (MIS). I have tried to highlight many real life situations in the Spotlight Feature, as appropriate illustrations of the concepts discussed. Emerging ideas like supply chain management, customer relationship management, electronic commerce are discussed with the prevalent practices in the industry. Case studies in the

Information system. Over the years, an information system has been considered a support function of key employed a major role in decision making. Now more and more organizations view information system in a new perspective.

An information system consists of four sections, namely, input, output, process and feedback as depicted in Figure 1.1. The input, usually consists of

Figure 1.1. Processing of an information system

captures raw data from the source that is immaterial of external or internal the information within the organization is internal and all other information is treated external. The input process converts the raw input into a meaningful form, and the processed information is the output to the recipients, employees and activities. For example, one input activity could be the login operation of a machine. Feedback from the output helps correct or manipulate the information to the input, so that the output conforms to the input. Companies, therefore, develop, maintain the information system through a feedback mechanism. Control is another activity in information management. We are more concerned here with the Computer Based Information Systems (CBIS), that those designed by computers in organized sector.

In information systems, another approach is the resource approach. The resource approach identifies the point at which the information becomes known and becomes useful for developing the application for the user.

Figure 1.2. Resource approach

In resource approach, the manipulation is done on the resource data. Data updates are done with the help of a process. The data is a resource to an organization. Maintenance of existing data is therefore more important *information system.* Over the years, an information system has been considered a support function, often one with a minor role in decision-making. Now more and more organizations view information system in a new perspective.

An information system consists of four activities, namely input, output, process and feedback as depicted in Figure 1.1. The input activity collects or

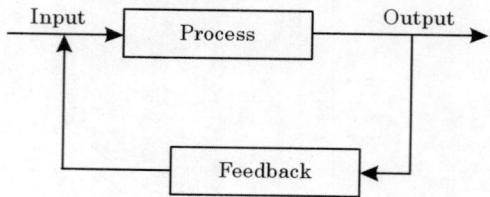

Figure 1.1 Functions of an information system.

captures raw data from the source that is in internal or external environment. The information within the organization is internal and all other information is treated external. The input process converts the raw input into a meaningful form and the processed information is the output to the recipients, employees and activities. For example, one output activity could be the tooling operation of a machine. Feedback from the output helps correct or manipulate the information to the input so that the output conforms to the input. Companies, therefore, develop or improve the information system through a feedback mechanism. Control is another activity in information management. We are more concerned here with the Computer Based Information Systems (CBIS) like the ones designed by companies in organized sector.

In information systems, another approach is the resource approach. The resource approach identifies the point at which the information becomes known and becomes useful for developing the application for the user.

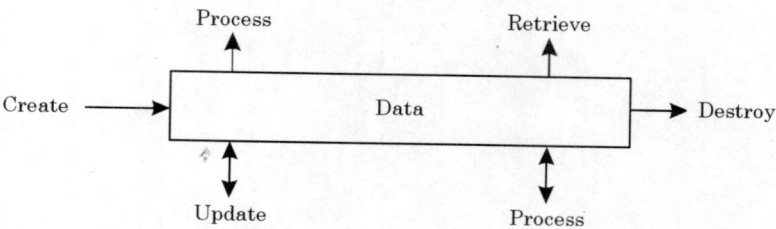

Figure 1.2 Resource approach.

In resource approach, the manipulation is done on the existing data. Data updates are done with the help of a process. The data is a resource to an organization. Maintenance of existing data is therefore more important today. Programs and software are useful only when the right data is available for processing.

> **SPOTLIGHT**
>
> In an accounting information system, all vouchers, cash books, bank bills, etc. are entered. These data are processed through computer to produce the output such as trial balance, balance sheet, sales register, etc. All vouchers, cash books, bank bills, etc. are the basic input or raw data. The process is developed and changed through a feedback system. So, the users of the system play a role in the feedback process. The outcome of the process is regulated through a control mechanism. The first approach is to create a system and later the resource. The existing data are updated year after year for further analysis.

Not all information has the same value. Information can be classified in many ways as per requirement. The same information has different values to different persons. For example, a ledger as an operation information is valuable to a junior accountant executive. At the same time, a senior level executive may not have interest in this on a regular basis. He may seek this information occasionally or as a special event. An information can be classified as *action* versus *no-action* information. In this case, the senior executive may receive the copy of ledger, but it is a *no-action* report to him.

Information can be *recurring* versus *non-recurring*. Information generated at a regular interval—like daily, weekly—is a recurring information. For example, trial balance is a piece of recurring information, whereas budget is non-recurring, generated once only at the beginning of the financial year. Information can be *internal* and *external*. Sales figures of last four years of an organization are available as internal information, whereas market share of all those companies manufacturing the same product is external information.

Good information must have the following characteristics:

- Accuracy
- Timeliness
- Less uncertainty
- An element of surprise value
- Should aid in decision-making
- Should update knowledge

The requirement of accuracy is self-explanatory. Erroneous information can lead to misleading conclusions. Information is a function of time, i.e.

$$I = f(t)$$

For example, information on inflation, index number and market shares is relevant only when it is up to date. Information technology helps here in presenting pertinent data in a timely manner to the user.

different in each organization, which depends on the type of products or services offered to customers. So, some organizations are highly technology oriented in terms of information system like banking, tourism and service sector. In some companies, such as call centres, medical transcription, etc. there would be no business transactions possible without the use of information technology. In manufacturing, these applications are used for production, inventory control, accounting procedures, quality control, etc. It is increasingly recognized that the best way to ensure that an organization is performing effectively, is to develop information architecture for company's information needs. It is a collection of all documents that represent a structure. The architecture shows the relationship of the parts to each other and to the whole, with respect to the business. It requires massive understanding to develop enterprisewide information architecture.

So, even organization has Standard Operating Procedures (SOPs), which are the precisely defined rules for accomplishing different tasks like writing an invoice, responding to customers, managing inventory, etc. An organization requires different kinds of people of different levels and specialities. Compared to the data workers (such as accountant, secretary), production or service workers (such as supervisor, foreman or packer), knowledge workers (such as programmer, scientist, engineer) have been gaining more importance. In today's context, all levels of management (senior, middle, operational) are expected to be creative to develop solutions for a broad range of problems. They need different pieces of information and information process systems. Otherwise due to evergrowing competition and economic pressure, business may be required as a norm rather than reengineering an exception. Business reengineering has a spectrum of goals to improve the business process. The results are continuous gradual improvements, such as Total Quality Management (TQM). Information technology is a critical enabler in this undertaking. So, information technology workers play a significant role in the Business Process Engineering (BPE). In many cases, the helm of control is with the Information Technology department.

Information technology is a multidisciplinary approach and the stakeholders are even the suppliers. Information Technology has changed the rules of business. Business has been following the same process, but it has changed the architecture. For example, supply chain is not new to business but the stakeholders have changed their roles with the help of information technology. There are many instances, where architecture was unthinkable, because of the infrastructure and the availability of technology to the end-user.

SPOTLIGHT

Timely delivery is the Unique Selling Proposition (USP) for a company in the courier business, which results in customer satisfaction. The information

> system can interact with the delivery and pickup processes. Once the material is delivered to the customer, the system updates the data within a few minutes. A customer can track the position of the material through a consignment number. In this case, the architecture and information system play vital roles. At the same time, in the process of delivery, reengineering is possible with the support of the technology.

1.3 TECHNOLOGY

Information technology is the glue that holds an organization together. The cost of technology decreases as application or usage increases. The cost of computer has decreased with the advancement in technology. Basically, a computer consists of hardware, software and storage unit. In addition, it has many input/output devices. Hardware is the physical equipment used for input, processing and output functions in an information system, such as central processing unit, keyboard, processor, etc. Chapter 3 describes computer hardware in detail.

Computer software consists of the detailed instructions or programs which coordinate and control hardware components in the information system. Application software (such as accounting, payroll) are examples of computer software. Storage technology includes physical media for storage (hard disk, floppy disk, etc.) and software programs governing the data on physical media. Telecommunication technology consists of both hardware and software that link various physical devices and transfers data from one location to another. The optical fibre is the medium through which data transmitted with very high speed and in least amount of time. E-mail is the outcome of the communication technology. Mobile commerce is not a distant dream today. The process of delivery of information and the quality of data or output has improved dramatically with the help of communication technology. Chapter 6 describes communication technology in detail.

Most corporations today would not be able to operate their businesses without computers. Even a small business depends heavily on information technology. Technology management is as important for their information system as it is for other functions like production. So the information system department plays the same kind of role in cost reduction activities as other departments do in a company. Technology has been changing. It is quite difficult to manage technology in an organization. Technology tracking is a part of every system analyst's job in any organization today. Tracking technology without any regard to the needs of the organization and business can waste a lot of time and money. Technology planners need to update their knowledge on new products and services. This knowledge helps technology planners:

2. Why should managers study information systems?
3. What is the relationship between an organization and a business? How has this relationship changed over time?
4. What is management process in an information system?
5. What are the management, organization and technology dimensions in an information system?
6. Discuss the functions of information systems.
7. "An information system consists of hardware and software"—Why is this statement inadequate?
8. What is Standard Operating Procedure (SOP)?

DISCUSSION QUESTIONS

1. Information Technology is the glue that holds organizations together. Discuss and comment.
2. Some people argue that problems with information systems will disappear when computers become faster and cheaper. Discuss and comment.
3. Information systems cannot solve some business problems. Discuss and comment.

2
Management Information Systems (MIS)

2.1 DEFINITION AND NEED

The field of Management Information Systems (MIS) is undergoing a profound change. Information technology is upsetting the basic assumptions which Management Information Systems (MIS) has served over the past forty years. Management Information Systems may not be fully based on computer. In the past, it stood well organized without the help of computers. A close analysis reveals that an MIS is not computer dependent in many areas. The MIS concept was based on processing data to present reports. Over the time, a lot of developments have taken place. Information is nothing but a product of data analysis. **Peter Keen** defined **MIS** as "the effective design, delivery and use of information system in an organization." In other words, MIS is the development and use of an effective information system.

Information management is one of the main functions in any organization. Organizations use tools to develop and analyze information. The emphasis lies on how information is to be structured and presented, which helps in decision-making process. So managements are concerned about how to manage the information system.

Over a period of time, when those conceptual developments were taking place, the concept of information technology emerged. So, organizations started computerization of information management. This concept brought a fundamental change in the working of MIS. The MIS became decentralized and a new kind of professionals emerged known as computer professionals. In that process, the concept of MIS changed to that of a decision-making system.

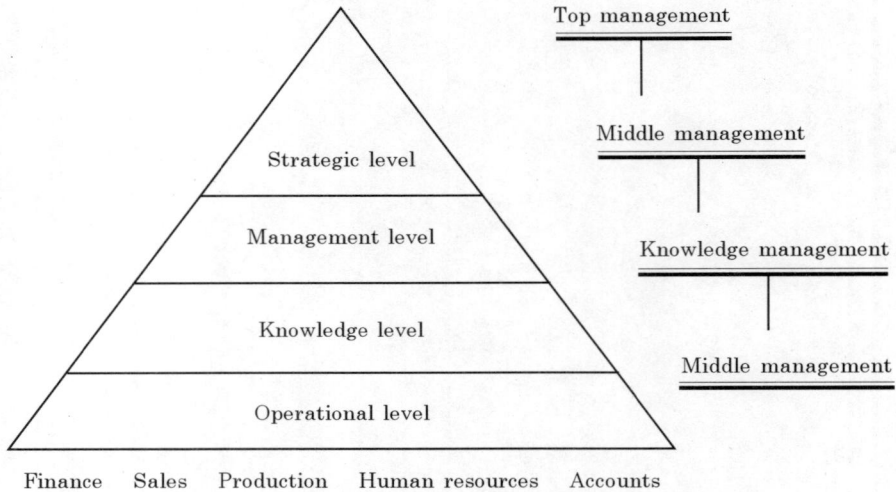

Figure 2.3 Types of information systems.

involve in sales, cash receipts, payroll, credits and flow of materials. The basic purpose at this level is to answer routine questions and track the flow of transactions in the organization. Examples of operational level systems include employee attendance system, record of bank deposit system in teller machines, stock management in stores, etc.

Knowledge level systems support the organization's data workers. The objective of the knowledge level systems is to help the organization to assimilate knowledge in the business and also to help the organization to manage paperwork. Today, office management machines have become increasingly popular in business applications.

Management level systems serve the administrative activities in the middle management and provide periodic reports rather than daily or instant information of operations. An example is the management of the cost of a project. In many cases, structured information may not be available or where the information is available, it may not be clear. In this case, the information may be emanating not only from the organization but also from outside. In similar cases, it is not possible to draw the data easily from the existing operational level. Thus management information systems support monitoring, controlling and decision-making processes at the managerial level.

The strategic level systems support the long-range planning activities, using both the internal and the external information. The principal objective is to help the organization in keeping pace with the environment. The forecasting of sales of a product in a manufacturing company is an example at the strategic level. As discussed, the knowledge management level gives a lot of inputs to the strategic management level. The top management— General Managers, CEO, Directors—is involved in the strategic level decision-making process.

Let us discuss specific categories of systems which exist in organizations and how organizations use these systems in business functions. Six major systems may exist in an organization:

- Transaction Processing System (TPS)
- Office Automation System (OAS)
- Knowledge Work System (KWS)
- Decision Support System (DSS)
- Management Information Systems (MIS)
- Executive Information System (EIS)

Figure 2.4 lists all the information systems showing their relationship with different sub-systems and how the system, in turn, is linked with different functional areas. In each level, examples from such functional areas are shown in the figure.

	STRATEGIC LEVEL SYSTEMS			
Executive support systems	Budget forecasting	Sales planning	Manpower planning	Production planning

	MANAGEMENT INFORMATION SYSTEMS				
Management information systems	Product costing	Sales management	Inventory management	Payroll management	Working capital management
Decision support systems	Cost analysis	Regional sales analysis	Production control	Overtime analysis	Capital cost analysis

	KNOWLEDGE LEVEL SYSTEMS				
Knowledge work systems	Data processing workstation	Attendance management machines			Graphics workstation
Office automation systems	Word processing	Document management	Mail management		Imaging system

	OPERATIONAL LEVEL SYSTEMS				
Transaction processing systems	Cash management	Distribution management	Shop floor materials management	Salary administration	Receivable management
	Finance	Sales	Production	Human resources	Accounts

Figure 2.4 Six major types of information systems.

Transaction processing system

This is the foundation of the organization at the operational level. The transaction processing system (TPS) deals with all kinds of data entry at any functional level and records the daily routine transactions necessary to conduct business. For example, in distribution management of the products, distribution data are entered into the computer once the products are distributed to the dealers. The data are entered in different locations of distribution at the time of data entry and processed from all locations. TPS example is discussed in detail in the Spotlight below. The whole distribution transaction processing system allows the organization to take decisions. Other examples of transaction processing system are receivable management, materials management in stores, shop floor production data administration, etc.

SPOTLIGHT

A company is in the business of manufacturing A4 size batteries used in torches, transistors, etc. and sells this product in rural areas. The product distribution chart is given below:

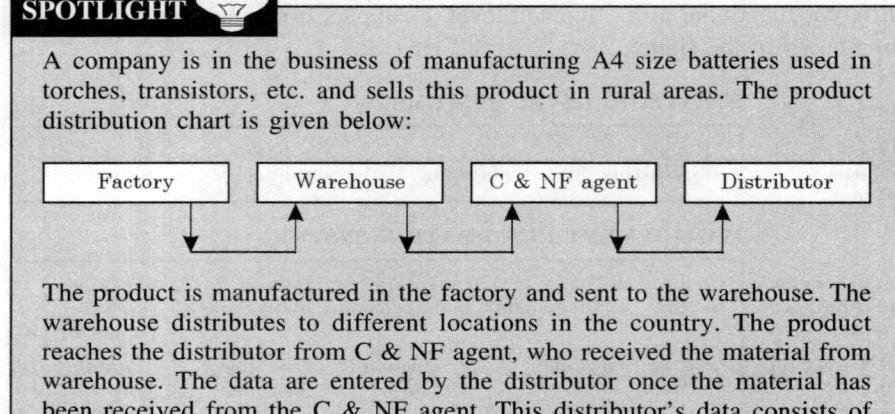

The product is manufactured in the factory and sent to the warehouse. The warehouse distributes to different locations in the country. The product reaches the distributor from C & NF agent, who received the material from warehouse. The data are entered by the distributor once the material has been received from the C & NF agent. This distributor's data consists of all information like C & NF agent, warehouse location, details of the product, etc. In the evening, at 5'o clock, all the distributors' data are sent to factory via the mailing system. Thus, the factory data are being updated daily. The transaction processing is taking place in different locations, in terms of the company, distributors and factory. It is an operational level job, where the logistics manager is involved in the whole transaction process.

Knowledge work system and office system

It serves the information needs at the knowledge level. The office automation system aids knowledge workers through automated system processing. Knowledge workers basically hold a formal degree in engineering or medicine or management, etc. They create knowledge and ensure that knowledge is properly integrated into the organization. Data workers who deal with the office automation system, on the other hand, are less educated and tend to depend on information rather than creating information. Office management systems handle and manage documents using document management software packages like word processing, image processing and digital filing, and schedule using electronic calendar and mail using electronic mail.

Management information systems

The term management information systems deals with a specific system, serving management level functions. MIS primarily serves the functions of controlling and decision-making at the managerial level. The executive deals with reports of all operations. The transaction processing data are represented through reports produced at regular intervals. In Figure 2.4, the examples shown are costing of product, sales management, inventory management, etc. Most MIS reports are routine-based and do not require analytical capability.

Decision support systems (DSS)

Decision support systems serves the management of the organization. Basically by design, DSS is more analytical than any other system. DSS is built of data, software and models. It is possible for the development of software packages to take decisions. For example, a ticket checking machine in a metro railway system does not require any human being for checking tickets. In an automated teller machine, money is delivered in an exact number of notes to the user. In both these cases, the machines take the decisions without any intervention from human beings. So models that are developed through study over a long time are implemented through machines. In many cases, DSS is interactive; the user can change assumptions and make other changes if required.

Executive support systems (ESS)

Executive support systems serves in the strategic level of information where senior managers are involved in decision-making process. In most of the cases, those decisions are non-routine and require judgement, evaluation and insight. The information or reports are not based on any agreeable procedure, as the source of data is outside the organization. For example, a change in the tax policy of the government of a country changes the balance sheet which, in turn, affects the shareholders' assets. The executive decisions in such cases are critical in nature, with inputs coming from management information systems as well. The emphasis is on the effort required to obtain information useful to the executives. Like other types of systems, ESS is not designed to assist specific needs but it provides a computerized environment which caters to the long-term requirement.

2.4 DEVELOPMENT OF MANAGEMENT INFORMATION SYSTEMS (MIS)

The development process of Management Information Systems (MIS) is linked with long-term business plans of the organization. As discussed earlier, Management Information Systems (MIS) requires resources like capital, time and capacity. The end result is information in the form of reports. Most of the organizations do not recognize information as a resource. They look at information just like a routine necessity. As an organization grows, the information also increases manifold. The Management Information Systems (MIS) plans are developed concurrent to the business plans. An organization of any size deals with numerous pieces of information.

Management Information Systems (MIS) may be developed in the following ways:
- Prototype method
- Life cycle approach

In the prototype method, initial methods are developed first. Once implemented, the system is refined and modified as per new specifications. This iterative process is followed till the system is accepted by the user.

In life cycle approach, the Management Information Systems (MIS) development is carried out through different phases. The phases are: Feasibility study, Analysis, Design, Implementation and Review.

In life cycle approach, apart from core areas, other systems like decision support system are also developed. The choice of Management Information Systems (MIS) design is decided on the basis of nature of the system and its applications. Thus the MIS is developed over time as the business increases. MIS depends on resources like hardware, software, and communication technology. It is, therefore, necessary to prepare the budget for MIS at the same time as the business plans.

The following chart shows how MIS can be developed in an organization. Today most organizations have Management Information Systems (MIS) departments, working with internal customers.

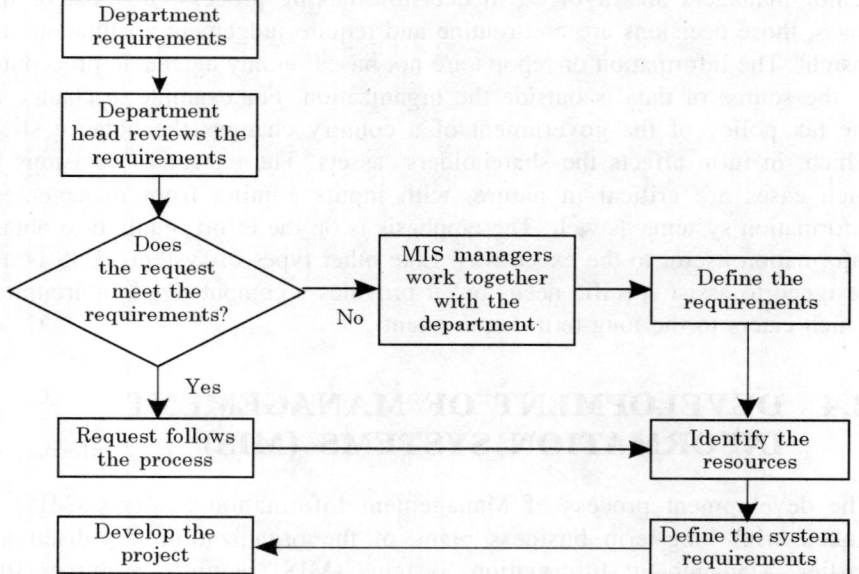

Figure 2.5 Management Information Systems (MIS) development model.

MIS development is a step-by-step process. Decision Support Systems (DSS) is interlinked with Management Information Systems (MIS). Software packages like Enterprise Resource Planning (ERP) are under that category. But the cost is very high compared to independent functional systems. Training and manpower development are the other areas which need continuous development. In many cases, companies fail to identify the cost benefits. The change in technology is also another area of concern in the development of Management Information Systems (MIS).

2.5 IMPLEMENTATION OF MANAGEMENT INFORMATION SYSTEMS (MIS)

Implementation of the Management Information Systems (MIS) is one of the major areas where the organizational transformation takes place. An organization usually develops MIS in-house. It is not an easy task to match the business goal with the implementation process. For example, the objective of a company may be to reduce the time interval between producing the bills and receiving the payments. In the process, the collection will improve and result in internal savings on working capital. The quarterly profit and loss account should reflect this increase in income or profit, even though the sales may be the same. The Management Information Systems may implement this process quarterly in phases. The whole implementation process is linked with other Management Information Systems (MIS) resources to be implemented as well. The lack of fulfilment in one area creates problems in another part. So, it is necessary to ensure that the problems in the organization are resolved first before the system is taken up for implementation.

In addition, some common problems occur in the area of human resource management. The resistance to MIS can occur within a group. It is also necessary to ensure that the MIS has the blessings of the management. Training to the users as well as all affected groups is an important area of concern. It allows employees to understand and accept the system much more easily. As a long-term measure, across-the-region based Management Information Systems (MIS), may be developed, if need be. But concurrent implementation of such requirements is definitely preferable.

REVIEW QUESTIONS

1. Discuss the levels of organization hierarchy in the light of information management.
2. What is TPS? How do TPS systems become effective to the organization?
3. Discuss the six major types of information systems with examples.

4. Describe the relationship between TPS, MIS, DSS and ESS.
5. What are the major components of MIS?
6. What is MIS? How are other discipline related to MIS?

DISCUSSION QUESTIONS

1. The Transaction Processing System (TPS) plays a major role in MIS. Discuss with examples.
2. Knowledge management systems are data driver processes. Express your views citing some examples.

3

Hardware

3.1 COMPUTER ARCHITECTURE

The architecture represents the backbone of a computer. In order to understand how a computer processes data, one needs to understand how the various components of a computer system function and what its capabilities to process data into information are. Once you finish reading this chapter, you should be in a position to understand the specifications of a computer as given below:

Processor 1.7 GHz/256 Internal cache/128 MB SDRAM/40 GB HDD/ 1.44 MB FDD/52X CD ROM Drive/32 MB 4X AGP Card/Onboard sound card/2 Serial ports; 1 Parallel port; 2 USB Ports/104 Keys; Keyboard/ Mouse/15" Colour monitor.

As illustrated in Figure 3.1, a computer consists of a Central Processing Unit (CPU) and four other devices, namely, secondary storage, input device, output device and communication device.

The Central Processing Unit manipulates raw data and controls other devices of the computer system. Storage devices feed data and program into central processor and store them for later use. The input device receives and converts data and instructions into electronic form and sends it to central processing unit. Output devices are connected to this electronic data and display this output in an understandable format.

A computer processes data (symbols, pictures or words) to a string of binary digits. A binary digit is called a **bit**, represents either a 'zero' (0) or a 'one' (1). The presence of an electronic or magnetic symbol means 'one' and the absence of the signal means a 'zero'. A string of eight (8) bits is called **byte** and can be used to represent a decimal number, a symbol or a character.

The computer can therefore represent all characters as groups of zeros

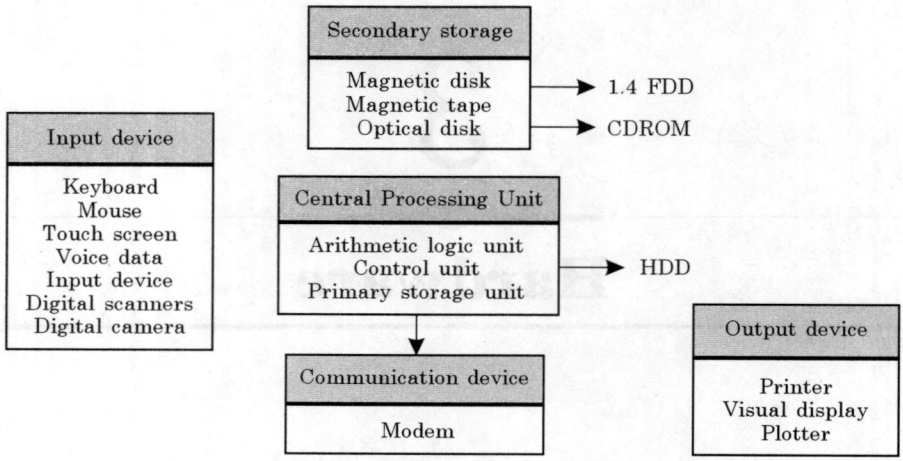

Figure 3.1 Components of a computer system.

and ones. This requirement led manufacturers of computers to develop standard binary codes. The computer can represent $2^8 = 256$ characters or symbols with the help of this binary code. There are two common codes available, namely, ASCII and EBCDIC. This code can represent every digit, alphabetic character or special character with 8 bits.

ASCII (American Standard Code for Information Interchange) was developed by the American National Standard Institute (ANSI) to provide a standard code that could be used by manufacturers in order to make all machines compatible with one another. ASCII was originally designed as a 7-bit code, but most computers use the 8-bit version of ASCII.

Microprocessor: This is a very large-scale integrated circuit with millions of transistors on a single chip. It integrates the computer's memory, logic and control on a single chip. Today, the microprocessor is widely used in personal computers in the 64-bit 1.77 megahertz chip, such as Intel Pentium4. The speed of the computer is measured in milliseconds.

Chips are measured in several ways such as 8-bit, 16-bit and 32-bit devices. This specification represents the number of bits that can be processed at one time by the machine and is referred to as word length. A 16-bit chip can process 16 bits or 2 bytes in a single machine cycle. The larger the word length, the greater the speed of the computer.

The second factor affecting the chip speed is the cycle speed. The control unit sets a beat to the chip so that the sequence of the event is followed logically, step by step. The beat is established by an internal clock and is measured in megahertz (MHz—millions of cycles per second). In the example given above, the machine clock speed is 1.17 MHz. Thus, the word length and the clock speed are the factors to be considered for selecting a computer, depending on the type of application in mind.

3.2 PROCESSING UNIT

The Central Processing Unit is part of the central processor where data manipulation occurs.

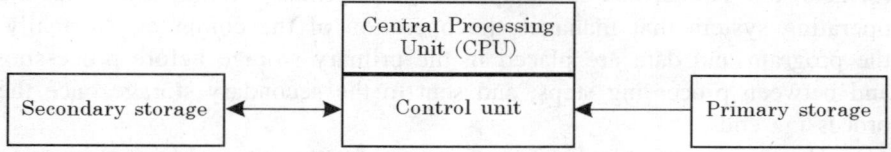

Figure 3.2 Processing unit.

The Central Processing Unit (CPU) consists of Arithmetic Logic Unit (ALU) and Control Unit. The control unit coordinates and controls other parts of the computer system. It brings one instruction at a time from memory and directs other components to perform the task. The control unit tells the input unit, what is to be read and where is it to be stored. It instructs the memory to store data in the specified address. The ALU receives instructions from the control unit such as which operations need to be performed, where to find the required data and where to store the results. The series of operations required to process a single machine instruction is called the machine cycle. It has two parts, an instruction cycle and an execution cycle.

The ALU performs the arithmetic operations such as addition, subtraction, multiplication and division. In addition, it also performs logical operations when one number is greater or less than another and when two are equal. This unit is also capable of matching characters. The ALU can perform logical operations on binary codes for letters as well as numbers.

SPOTLIGHT

> In a medicine shop, the accounts clerk checks the price of two similar kinds of products manufactured by two different companies. He checks the register and looks for comparison. It is the arithmetic and logic unit of a computer that performs this act of "matching characters".

3.3 STORAGE

The storage unit is one of the main parts in a computer system. The processing job is performed on data, which is stored for immediate application or future use. Size, like speed, is an important consideration in a system. Information is stored in a computer in binary form that is 0s and 1s. Bits together form bytes, which we have discussed earlier. One byte can be used to store one character like 'A'. One thousand bytes together (actually

1024 bytes) are called a kilobyte (kB). Each megabyte is approximately 1 million bytes. One gigabyte is equal to one billion bytes (approximately).

In Figure 3.2, the CPU is attached to primary and secondary memory. The primary memory has three functions. It stores all parts of the program (or data) that is executed or manipulated. The primary storage also holds the operating system that manages the operation of the computer. Normally, the program and data are placed in the primary storage before processing and between processing steps, and sent to the secondary storage once the processing ends.

How is it possible for an electronic device like primary storage to actually store information? The internal primary storage is called Random Access Memory (RAM). It is called RAM because it can directly access any randomly chosen location in the same amount of time. The primary memory is divided into memory cells. Each memory cell has an individual address indicating where it is located in RAM. The program resides in the memory of RAM at the time of execution. So the more the RAM the more is the power of computing. Today any personal computer can support 16 MB to 256 MB RAM. The cost of the computer is dependent upon the size of the RAM. Since the cost of RAM has also come down, it is better to have more RAM memory provided it is supported by the microprocessor. The personal computer can be upgraded from 16 MB to 524 MB RAM.

RAM is used for short-term storage of data and programs. RAM is volatile: the contents of RAM are lost when the computer is turned off or electric supply is disrupted by a power outage.

Another type of primary memory, called Read Only Memory (ROM), contains instructions or data that cannot be changed or removed; but only can be read. ROM chips come from the manufacturers with embedded programs stored in them. ROM chips are the storage of the manufacturer's specific codes such as the Basic Input Output System (BIOS) chip used in a personal computer. It is not generally programmable by the user. Every time we start a computer, ROM displays information like the name of the manufacturer, set-up keys, etc. There are two other subclasses of ROM chip. One is Programmable Read Only Memory (PROM) and the other is Erasable Programmable Read Only Memory (EPROM). They can be programmed once. In a typical conveyor belt manufacturing system, the control panel stores data on a PROM. EPROM chips are used for device control, such as robots, where the programs have to be changed on a rotation basis with the EPROM chip. The program can be erased and reprogrammed.

A register is another kind of the fastest and most expensive memory where small amounts of data and instructions reside for thousandths of a second just prior to use. The cache memory is another kind of high-speed storage of frequently used instructions and data. Both kinds of memories are costlier than RAM and all programs do not support it. In a PC, normally 256 K cache memory is available.

Most of the information stored by storage devices such as disks and tapes is located outside the primary storage area. Primary storage is composed of semiconductor memories. All data and programs are stored in the computer, which is outside the CPU, and is known as secondary storage. The cost of secondary storage is low and constitutes the maximum part of the storage system. This media can transfer large amount of data rapidly to the CPU. But since secondary storage requires mechanical movement to gain access to the data, in contrast to primary storage, it is relatively slow.

Magnetic tape is a magnetically coated strip of plastic on which data can be encoded. It supports large storage capacity ranging from a few hundred KB to several GB. It is much slower than any other secondary media.

Digital Audio Tape (DAT) is a type of magnetic tape that uses an indigenous scheme called helical scans to record data. A DAT cartridge is slightly larger than a credit card and contains a magnetic tape that can hold from 2–20 gigabytes of data. The most common format for DAT cartridges is Digital Data Storage (DDS) which is the industry standard for Digital Audio Tape formats. Both the above types of storage are usually not available with the personal computer (PC).

The most widely used secondary storage medium today is the magnetic disk, i.e. the floppy disk and the hard disk drive. Microcomputers use floppy disks that are flat, 5.25 inch or 3.5 inch disk of polyester film with magnetic coating. The 3.5 inch disk has a capacity range of 400 KB–1.4 MB. Hard disks are thin steel platters with an iron oxide coating. The term 'hard' is used to distinguish it from a soft floppy disk. A single hard disk usually consists of several platters. Each platter requires two read/write heads, one for each side. Each platter has the same number of tracks, and the track location that cuts across all platters is called a cylinder. The storage capacity range is from 10 MB to several in a microcomputer. The data transfer speed is higher in the hard disk, than in the other kind of media discussed so far.

The optical disk, also called the compact disk or laser optical disk, stores data at densities many times greater than those of magnetic disks and are available with microcomputers. Data are recorded on optical disks when a laser device burns microscopic pits in the reflective layer of a spiral track. An optical disk can store large quantities of data, not only text but also pictures, sound and full motion video, in a highly compact form. A laser beam from an optical head reads the optical disk by scanning the disk. The most common optical disk system is called Compact Disk Read Only Memory or CD-ROM. It can store up to 650 MB and it is read only storage. Write Once, Read Many or the WORM optical disk system allows users to record data only once on an optical disk. Once written, the data cannot be erased, but can be read indefinitely. One of the important features of the CD-ROM is the speed of the CD. CD-ROM players are generally classified as single speed or some multiples of single speed player. For example, a 52X CD-player accesses data at four times the speed of a single speed player. But there are so many variations. Also, you need to be aware of whether the CD-ROM uses the Constant Linear Velocity (CLV) or Constant Angular Velocity (CAV) technology. Rewritable CD drives are available at a lower price. So the demand for VCD/DVD has increased a lot. Even computers are loaded with VCD writable drive. We cannot write on CD-ROMs. One has to buy read-write CDs for this purpose.

The selection of computer for different types of applications is not an easy task. The differences in the size, speed, and compatibility are the major areas of concern. The components that we have discussed earlier are available in different types and makes. So, the CPU fails to utilize its capacity to the maximum level. Configuration of a computer is also important from the point of view of input and output devices. Software and programs also play a vital role on the selection of a computer.

3.4 COMPUTER TYPES

Based on the size and processing capabilities, the contemporary classifications of computers are:

- Mainframe
- Minicomputer
- Workstation
- Microcomputer
- Supercomputer

The **mainframe** is a large computer with massive memory and high processing power. It is used for large commercial and scientific applications, which require with huge data and complicated processing. IBM Enterprise System 9000 is an example of a mainframe, having 50 megabytes to over 1 gigabyte of Random Access Memory (RAM).

A minicomputer is the middle-range computer with about 10–650 megabyte of Random Access Memory (RAM). DEC VAX 7000, MODE 600 are examples of this category. A **microcomputer** is one that can be placed on a desktop or be portable with 640 kilobytes–256 megabytes of RAM. Intel PIV is the example of this category.

Workstation is more powerful and has more processing capability than a microcomputer. Commercial users use workstations. However, the distinction between microcomputers and workstations is now blurring. The principal reason is that the microprocessors used in PCs are now as powerful as many of those used in workstations.

A **supercomputer** is a highly sophisticated and powerful machine that is used for tasks which require extremely rapid and complex calculations with hundreds or thousands of variable factors. Supercomputers have traditionally been used in scientific and military works. For example, Y-MP/C90 made by Cray Research Inc. can perform 2.1 billion mathematical calculations per second.

The term microcomputer is sometimes used synonymously with the personal computer since micros were primarily intended for personal or single user. Today micros can operate in a single-user personal computer as a stand-alone system or as part of a workstation in a network system. The configuration shown in Figure 3.1 is an example of a microcomputer.

3.5 INPUT/OUTPUT DEVICES

Interaction with a computer system is possible mainly through input and output devices. As mentioned earlier, the performance depends on the peripherals attached to the computer. So, the selection of input and output devices is another important criterion. Input/output devices are also called peripheral devices.

The traditional method of data entry is through keyboard. The keyboard is an input device, which has different types of keys for data entry, like numeric, alphabetic and special keys. A keyboard is connected to a computer through a port.

The mouse is a device that controls the movement of the cursor or pointer on the screen. The 'point and click' actions of the computer have made it an increasingly popular alternative to keyboard and text-based commands. Multimedia graphic packages help to draw images quickly. Serial mouse is connected directly to an RS-232 or a PS/2 port. Normally two serial ports are attached to the computer. It is desirable to connect a mouse through the PS/2 port, available with the computer. The cordless mouse is connected through infrared or radio waves.

The trackball is another kind of device, fixed with the system. Trackballs are the popular pointer devices for laptop or portable computers.

A joystick is similar to the mouse, except that with a mouse, the cursor moving stops as soon as you stop moving the mouse. Joysticks are, however, used mostly in computer games.

The touch screen is easy to use as an input device. A user can enter limited amount of data by touching the surface of a sensitized video display monitor with a pointer. Touch screens are in common use at retail stores, metro stations, railway reservation counters, etc.

Source data automation captures data in a computer in a readable form from the source. The application varies from retail stores, libraries to banking systems. The applications are error free and need less human interaction. Source data automation permits information about events to be captured directly and indirectly. These principal source data automation technologies are Magnetic Ink Character Recognition (MICR), Optical Character Recognition (OCR), pen-based input, digitizers and voice input.

MICR technology is primarily used in cheque processing for the banking industry. The number written on the bottom of a cheque is printed with a special kind of ink. A Magnetic Ink Character Recognition reader translates the characters on the cheques and sends to the bank for processing into a digital form for the computer. Another application area is the employee identity card in an organization.

The OCR device translates the specially designed marks, characters and codes into a digital form. Bar code is the most widely used optical code and is used at point-of-sale locations in supermarkets, libraries, transportation facilities, etc.

Hand-writing recognition devices such as pen-based 'tablet', 'notebooks' or 'note pads' are input technologies, especially for people working in the sales or service areas. These pen-based input devices usually consists of a flat screen display tablet and a pen-like stylus. In this pen-based input, users directly print into a table-sized screen; the inputs are converted into a digital form, so that they can be stored or processed and analyzed. The technology requires special pattern-recognition software to accept pen-based input instead of keyboard input.

The scanner is an input device that converts images such as pictures or documents into a digital form that computer can interact. Today, the scanner is an essential component in image processing industry. Optical scanners do not distinguish text from illustrations; they represent all images in bit maps. But other types of formats like JPEG, MPEG are also available. Thus, photographs and images scanned are manipulated through photoshop packages. Images can be input into computers using a digital camera. By this process, the digital camera takes a still photograph, stores it and then sends it as a digital input into the computer. The images are then stored as digital files.

The voice recognition system has been gaining success in the industry. Voice input devices convert spoken words into digital form. The voice recognition software compares the electrical patterns produced by the speaker's voice with a set of pre-recorded patterns.

The processor sends reports to the users through the output devices. The output device helps the user to receive the data or output from the computer. Output devices include Visual Display Unit (VDU), printer, loudspeaker, plotter, etc.

The VDU or monitor is basically a Cathode Ray Tube (CRT) terminal. It works much like a television picture tube, with an electronic 'gun' shooting a beam of electrons to illuminate the pixels on the screen. Monitors can be classified according to their display capabilities. Typical CRTs display 80 columns and 25 lines of text data. The size of the monitor is also an important issue. The monitors normally used for desktop application are of 14 inch size. Monitors of size 16 inch or more are often called full-page monitors.

The digital monitor receives input from the video adaptor. Most commonly used adaptors are Video Graphics Array (VGA) and Super Video Graphic Array (SVGA). Black and white monitors are used for Monochrome

Display Adaptor (MDA). The pictures on the monitor are made of dots, which are known as pixels. The resolution of a monitor indicates the number of pixels displayed on the monitor. The colours or shades depend on the number of bits used to represent the pixels. An 8-bit colour monitor uses 8 bits for each pixel, making it possible to display $2^8 = 256$ different colours. The quality of a monitor largely depends on its resolution, i.e. how many pixels can it display and how many bits are used to represent each pixel. Video Graphics Array or VGA monitors display 640 by 480 or about 300,000 pixels. In contrast, Super Video Graphics Array or SVGA monitors display 1024 by 768 or nearly 800,000 pixels. The colour monitors use 24 bits per pixel, allowing them to display more than 16 million different colours. This requires more computer memory but permits finer details and the ability to produce any kind of image on the display screen.

Printers produce the hardcopy of the output. Printers are of two types—impact and non-impact. Impact printers comprise daisy wheel, dot matrix and inkjet, while laser printers are of non-impact type. Most printers print only one character at a time but some printers can print an entire line or page at a time. Daisy wheel printers produce print letters of high quality type like the ball-head typewriter. The speed is, however, very slow compared to all other types. Moreover the product is not available for commercial use nowadays. Dot matrix printers are impressive and fast also but do not produce high-quality output. Speed and quality are two important characteristics of dot matrix printers.

Speed, normally denoted as characters per second (CPS), can vary from 300 to 1200 characters per second. Characters, graphics are printed by striking pins. The quality depends on the number of pins, which can vary from 9–24. In addition, printers are also available on 80 and 132 columns per page. It handles up to 4-part form (1 original + 3 copies) for printing bills, challan copies.

Multimedia is a part of the computer system. Presentations are prepared with the help of pictures and sound. The speaker is an output device. The quality of sound depends on the speaker and the sound card inside the computer. But one should remember that the quality of the computer depends on the multimedia software as well.

The discussion will not be complete without mentioning the modem. The device used to convert the digital signal into an analog signal and conversely from analog signal to a digital signal, is a **mo**dulator/**dem**odulator or **modem**. A modem is used when the data generated by a computer which is digital is to be transmitted over the telephone network, which is analog. A modem can be external or internal. The external modem is connected with the serial port connection. The speed of the data transfers available is 56 K, but the actual speed depends on the speed of data permissible by the telephone company.

SPOTLIGHT

In the railway reservation system, one of the major jobs is printing of tickets for reservation. The ticket is a pre-printed material with blank spaces for printing information like PIN, coach details, age, train number, etc. The quality is not so important because all prints are text in nature. Here size, text quality and speed are the factors. An 80-column dot-matrix and 24 pins with 300 characters per second (CPS) printers can be used for this purpose.

In the selection of an inkjet printer, the following points need to be checked before purchase:

Photo quality: The manufacturer claims photographic quality output, but an inkjet printer requires a special photo-ink cartridge.

High resolution: Print's resolution is measured in dots per inch (dpi)—the indicator of print quality. Higher resolution tends to mean sharper text, the capability to use smaller fonts and better quality graphics. Other factors such as ink-dot size, shape and placement also contribute to print quality.

Fastest print speed: The best colour printer can print twelve pages per minute. However, the manufacturers tend to rate their colour printing speed on the basis of using black text or simple colour test patterns.

Best ink system: Select a printer that can hold both colour and black ink cartridges. A four colour (CMYK—Cyan, Magenta, Yellow, Black) or a six colour (also known as photo ink) printer is recommended. This does not cost too much but the colour will be sharp.

Managing running costs: The best photo quality is obtained with special photo papers; a good quality printer should be able to deliver acceptable photo quality prints on plain papers. It is recommended to buy a printer that can be used for everyday plain paper printings to 'make-or-break' boardroom presentations.

Ease of use: The last things to consider are difficult set-up, software incompatibility, driver setting and connections.

Multi-user: In today's multi-user and multi-platform computing environment, it is better to have a flexible printer, compatible with personal computer. The Universal Serial Bus (USB) port is fast gaining popularity for its convenience. The user avails the benefit of a free parallel port for other purposes, where the printer is connected to the Universal Serial Bus (USB) port.

Inkjet printers work by spraying ionized ink at a sheet of paper. Inkjet printers print high quality printings and provide a resolution of 1200 dots per inch (dpi). The cartridges and paper are expensive. So the recurring cost is high. Higher resolution means sharper text of a good quality. A 1440 dots dpi inkjet can print at 720 or 360 dpi when printing low-resolution graphics or text.

Laser printers fall under the category of the non-impact printers. A laser printer utilizes a laser beam to produce an image on a drum. The laser light charges the drum, which is rolled through a reservoir or toner and picks up the charged portion of the drum. Finally, the toner is transferred to the paper through a combination of heat and pressure. The available resolution varies from 300–1200 dpi. The printing quality is better than that provided by inkjet printers. The speed of laser printer ranges from 4–20 pages of text per minute (TPM). All laser printers come with RAM and one can increase the memory if required. A significant amount of memory is required to print high-resolution graphics.

Plotter draws pictures, texts on paper. The size of the paper is the major issue in the plotter. The application of plotter is restricted to engineering drawings.

A voice output converts digital output data back into intelligible speech. Sounds are pre-recorded, coded and stored in disks, to be translated back as spoken words. A sound-card is required to enable the system to produce sounds.

The configuration of a laptop computer is listed here:

P IV M 1.8 GHZ, 256 MB DDR, 20 GB HDD, 24 × CD ROM
LAN + MODEM, 35.8 cm (14.1″) TFT, Li-Ion-battery.

The laptop computer works at fast speed and offers all the features of a desktop computer. The basic benefit is that it is portable, can also run on battery and uses thin flim transistor (TFT) screen. The cost is comparatively much higher than that of a desktop machine. It is also possible to connect it to networks and the Internet. There are inbuilt internal modem and network card, etc. It supports all kinds of printers and software.

Advancements in computer science and manufacturing techniques promise to maintain a historic growth pattern in the hardware industry. Reports of different journals and magazines over the last thirty years show that computer costs have reduced by a factor of ten per decade, and capability has increased by a factor of at least hundred per decade. This momentum is likely to be maintained. The cost of a computer, compared to the power of computing, has come down drastically. Today's microprocessors palm top size can perform high level computations.

REVIEW QUESTIONS

1. What are the components of a computer system?
2. Distinguish between a bit and a byte.

3. Name and define the measure of storage capacity of computer.
4. Name the major components of Central Processing Unit (CPU).
5. List and describe the major types of input devices.
6. List and describe the major types of output devices.
7. Describe how information is stored in memory of a computer.
8. Name and describe the factors that affect the speed and the performance of a computer.
9. What are the differences between a mainframe and a minicomputer?
10. What is computer configuration?
11. Describe the output storage unit of a computer.
12. What is a workstation?

DISCUSSION QUESTIONS

1. Large computers such as mainframes have no future. Comment on this statement.
2. The useful life of a personal computer is about one and half years. Comment and discuss.
3. It is better to lease a personal computer rather than buy it. What factors would you consider in deciding whether to buy or to lease a PC.

4
Software

4.1 OPERATING SYSTEM AND SYSTEM SOFTWARE

In the last twenty years or so, organization and media are increasingly using advanced computer hardware. But without the help of software, the computer revolution would not have been possible. The computer hardware is useless and cannot perform any tasks without software. This chapter deals with software and explains how software turns computer hardware into a useful information system management. Communication with hardware is not possible without software. **Software** is a detailed set of instructions that controls and manages the operations of a computer system. The functions of a software package are:

1. to manage the various resources of the organization,
2. to provide tools to human beings to take advantages of those resources, and
3. to act as an intermediary between stored data and organization.

A series of statements or instructions that are written to perform a specific job is known as a software program. The process of writing the program is termed **programming** and the individuals who perform job are called **programmers**.

The stored program concept means that the programs are stored in the hard disk or primary memory with other data. The stored programs are executed as required by the user. There are mainly three types of software packages (Figure 4.1):

- System software
- Application software
- End-user software.

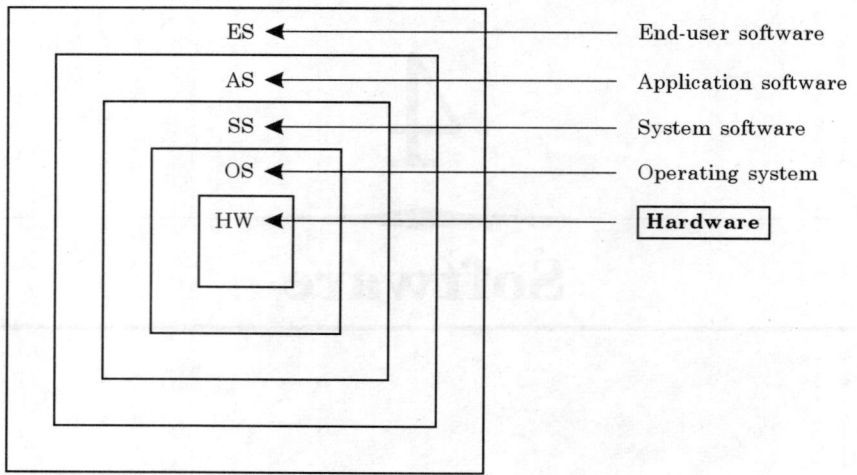

Figure 4.1 Software system.

It would now be evident that communication with the computer is possible only through software. All those input and output devices can communicate with the user only with the help of a software. So, there is a set of generalized programs, known as **system software**, that manage the resources of the computer such as CPU, and communicate with other peripherals and devices. **Application software** is written for or by the users to perform a specific task. The job of application software is not to communicate with the printer but to process a task such as a mailing list. Thus, system software coordinates between the various parts of the computer, its peripherals and mediates between application software and computer hardware.

The **operating system** is also a system software that performs functions like allocation and assignment of system resources, scheduling the use of computer resources and monitoring the computer system activities. The operating system allocates resources to the application job in the execution queue. It provides locations of memory and controls the input and output devices. Most of the operating system is stored in the hard disk, to which primary storage has very rapid access. The device on which the computer operating system is stored is called the system device.

4.2 MULTIPROGRAMMING, MULTIPROCESSING AND TIME SHARING

It is possible to share a computer system through concurrent use of a CPU, that is, only one program uses the CPU at any given moment but the input/output needs of other programs can be serviced at the same time. Two or more programs are active at the same time but they do not use the same computer resources simultaneously. With multiprogramming, a group of programs takes turns using the processor.

Multitasking allows more than one program to run concurrently—to execute more than one task at the same time. The terms multitasking and multiprocessing are often used interchangeably, although in multitasking, only one CPU is involved, it switches from one program to another so quickly that the users do not understand the difference. Multiprocessing, sometimes implies that more than one CPU is involved.

Time-sharing is an operating system capability when many users can share computer-processing capabilities simultaneously. In this case, the CPU spends a fixed amount of time on one program before moving to another. Each user is allocated a fixed time. The user is free to perform any operation and when he finishes, another user is given time.

The problems faced in multiprogramming have led to the development of the concept of virtual storage. Virtual storage handles programs more efficiently because the computer divides the program into smaller lengths and stores the small portions into the memory. In live, when the program is running, a certain part of the main memory remains unutilized, because the programs add up to less than the total amount of primary storage available. Virtual storage takes advantage of this feature of processing. Virtual storage breaks a program into separate segments called pages. So, a very large number of programs can reside in primary memory, such as only one page of each program is actually located there. In this chapter, we would restrict ourselves to microcomputer in the study of operating system. The networking operation system will be discussed in the respective chapter. Since a lot of changes have taken place in the software technology products, it is not important to understand them from the basics. One operation system software may be superior to the others in many aspects, but the basic difference depends on the availability of the product. The developments in hardware technology have also made the software more complicated. So, the Operating System (OS) software, which is not in a position to support a new kind of hardware, has become obsolete. In this chapter, we will deal with software available presently in the industry. Multitasking is one of the principal strengths of operating system for microcomputers. The Disk Operating System (DOS) was the operating system in early 1970s. Today all computers are equipped with the Graphical User Interface (GUI) base operating system. The operating system interacts with graphic icons, and mouse is used for making selections. Microsoft Windows is a highly popular graphical user interface that runs in conjunction with the DOS. It has various versions available in the market. Windows XP is one of the most popular operating systems. The latest product is Windows Vista with many new features compared with the earlier versions.

The operating system plays the role of the interpreter with the computer. The machine communicates through the operating system

PC-DOS is a product under the disk operating system category. Here the users have to remember commands to communicate with the machine. The screen displays a prompt like **C:>**. Here C denotes for C drive under root or main directory. Once a subdirectory is selected, it looks **C \ Note :>**. Again Note is the subdirectory under root directory C. Once one changes the drive, the screen will display accordingly like B:>. Here B is the drive. DOS consists of two kinds of commands—internal and external. Internal commands are copy, delete, CD, Rd, DIR, etc. CHKDSK, DISKCOPY, EDIT, BACKUP, RESTORE are examples of external commands. COMMAND.COM executes an internal file. For external command, each command requires one file, like edit.Exe. DOS was upgraded to different versions up to 6.20. In the early 1990s, Windows was introduced in the market. It was a graphical user interface. Users do not require to remember all commands, mouse is the input device with a keyboard. It consists of icons on the desktop. Each icon has its own meaning like recycle bin, my computer, etc. Recycle bin stores files once deleted from the directory. It is possible to send back the deleted files to the directory if required. The delete process in Windows consists of two stages. But in DOS, once deleted, the files are deleted forever. There were other operating systems available like OS/2 by IBM. But those products have lost their market potential over time.

Microsoft Windows has been upgraded to different versions over a period of time. The different versions are named Windows 95, Windows 98, Windows 2000, Windows ME, Windows XP, now Windows Vista. Each version was upgraded with additional features or existing features were enhanced. For example, the file management system has been upgraded in each version with added features. The control panel has got a new look over time. Like printer management, file installation, network management, internet explorer were upgraded in different versions. It is important to remember that each version required more random access memory and had disk space to install the operating system. It allows to customize desktop as per user requirements. In graphical user interface-based operating system, 'drag and drop' facility is the special characteristic. Let us take one small example to differentiate between the disk operating system and the graphical user interface-based operating system.

C:>COPY C : Book.DBF A: ↵

This command copies the file Book.DBF from C drive to A drive. But in Windows, the command is, select the file and send to A drive. The users do not need to write and recall commands in the second case. But in graphical user interface based software, one has to remember the steps.

In DOS, without knowing the command, operation is not available. But in GUI-based systems, one can click any icon without any prior knowledge.

The operating software handles other issues in addition to file management. The machine will not work, if the operating system is not installed properly. The computer may not start in case the OS installation is improper. Users need to understand OS before the installation of other software products. Manufacturers are selling OS with the computer.

The installation of operating system requires training and experience, especially for customized installation. But OS is a self-running process at the time of installation. Nowadays, compared to floppy disk, the CD has made it easier to install the operating system. The caveat is that one must look carefully at the hardware configuration before installation. It is recommended that all instructions should be carefully read before installation; otherwise, the computer may not start after installation, and it is a very cumbersome process to recover.

Selecting an operating system for a microcomputer depends on the application of the computer in the organization. It should be easy to install the operating system and also easy to use. The user interface features of the operating system should be easy to learn. The operating system should be able to run multiple applications without causing a crash of the machine. The compatibility is another important criteria for the selection of OS. The hardware or the input/output devices should be compatible with the operating system, that is, they should function properly with actual performances. It is always better to check the OS compatibility before buying new devices. Otherwise, the OS may fail to recognize the devices. Another area of concern is the upgradation of the operating system. For example, it is possible to upgrade Windows 98 to Windows XP. But converting it to a lower level is a cumbersome process. The upgrading may not support the devices attached to the computer. It is advisable to check with the vendor before installing a new operating system.

4.3 PROGRAMMING LANGUAGE AND UTILITY SOFTWARE

All kinds of software running in the computer system are written in a form, which is understandable to the computer, known as **language**. There are many languages available under different applications. In the beginning, it was much more difficult to communicate with the computer. Over a long period, many languages have been developed, which are easy to write and learn. To communicate with the first-generation computers, programmers had to write programs in machine language using 0s and 1s of of binary code. So, specialized programmers were required who could think, understand and work directly in the machine language of a computer. The second-generation programming languages were assembly languages. Here the programmers substituted words with certain mnemonics such as "add", "sub", "load", etc. A language translator converts the language statements (like English) into machine language. Programming languages like the natural language entered into third-generation computers through the development of several high-level languages. High-level languages help to reduce the number of details and concentrate more on logic to solve the problems. The languages used initially were languages such as FORTRAN, COBOL, etc. Fourth-generation computer languages emerged in the late 1970s. These languages dramatically reduced the programming time and the dependence of users on the programmers. Fourth-generation tools also include pre-written software for direct use, known as **packages**. For example, Microsoft EXCEL users can create their own financial data and manipulate data without programmers' intervention. Fourth-generation languages may be categorized into several kinds of application development tools, such as query language, application generators, financial planning language, etc. Query generation languages allow users to search a database using certain selective commands. Structured Query Language (SQL) is very popular under this category. The fifth-generation languages are in development stage. Natural languages are still in development stages, but they promise to contribute mainly to two areas, which are (a) artificial intelligence and (b) expert systems.

So far we have discussed different generations and the languages developed. The basic question is how does a computer understand those languages? Most of the third- and fourth-generation languages are written in standard English or other readable forms. So, the computer must convert these human-readable instructions into a form, which it can understand. The system software includes special language that translates higher-level languages into machine language, which computer can execute. Those types of system software are called compiler or interpreter. Before translation, these high-level language programs are called source code. The compiler translates this source code to machine code called the object code. The object code modules are joined together with other object code modules in a process just before execution called linkage editing (Figure 4.2).

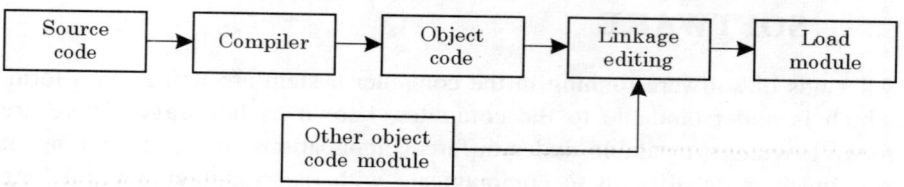

Figure 4.2 The compilation and execution process.

Some languages do not support the compiler but support the interpreter, which translates each statement, one at a time, into machine code and executes it.

A new area in software development, to meet the need of business to fashion systems that are flexible and quick, is the object-oriented programming tool. Traditional software development methods have treated data and procedures separately as independent components. Object-oriented programming combines data and the specific procedures that operate on those data into one object. The object combines the data and the program codes. Instead of passing data to procedure, the program sends a message for an object to perform a procedure that is already embedded into it. The same message may be sent to many different objects but each will implement the message differently. Because an object's data are encapsulated from other parts of the system, each object is an independent software building block that can be used in many different systems without changing the programming code. It reduces the time to write programming code by producing reusable software or programming code. The success of Internet-based applications has given a new dimension to object-oriented programming. Languages like Java and C++ have the property of object-oriented technology.

The trend in language software shows that easy-to-use and compatibility with hardware devices are here to stay in this industry. The languages are the basic raw materials to develop software. The challenges lie in development of new application tools like speech-recognition software, virtual programming, special activity software and their applications in the industry. Success of any language will depend on its development potential with pre-defined time frame of the user.

4.4 END-USER AND OFFICE AUTOMATION

Application software is primarily concerned with accomplishing the tasks of end-users. Many different programming languages can be used to develop different types of application software. The end-users are directly involved with computers. In a railway reservation system, the data entry operator is the direct end-user. In addition to that, the system delivers Management Information Systems (MIS) reports to the other end-users. So the application software may be considered a readymade solution to the user. The program or application software is developed and loaded to the user front. We can categorize mostly all kinds of software used as direct application for specific purpose or application software. An application software is a pre-written, pre-coded program that eliminates the need for individuals or organizations to write their own software programs for certain day-to-day functions. An application software is also known as **software package**. The majority of package software available in the market is application software. These packages are available for a large number of major business applications. They may also contain customized features tailored as per user's requirements. Although technical experts must install application packages for a large complex system, many application packages can be installed directly by the end-users. Office automation softwares like Word, Excel, and PowerPoint constitute one category, whereas Computer Aided Design (CAD)/Computer Aided Manufacturing (CAM) softwares constitute another category for drawing and design environment. Payroll application software, financial packages, taxation applications are another general category of software. There are also several other numerous types of application software available for different industry and product category.

The focus of software industry is on application software. An Operating System normally supports all types of application software. The basic focus of computerization is on the application part. The automation in manufacturing industry is running with the help of software. The application software can, therefore, be categorized in the following manner:

(a) Readymade
(b) Customized
(c) Embedded

Readymade softwares are office suite softwares such as document management, spreadsheet, e-mail, presentation software, etc. Financial accounting packages, payroll software and market research packages are part of another type in the readymade segment. Small and medium size organizations rely on readymade application software. Multimedia software is available as a readymade product. Document development software has been gaining market under this category. As a result, training institutions offer courses on readymade packages. The trained manpower is also available.

Customized segment is the largest category. The software business has the maximum share under this category. Companies, basically large manufacturing companies, multinationals, blue-chip stocks/companies are increasingly working with the customized software. The software products are developed as per their requirement in the business. Two companies in the same business may have two different software packages running in the accounts department. The customized software allows flexibility to change, which is not easily avail-able in the case of readymade software. In manufacturing, different processes are run by application software. The conveyor belt line in an assembly line, auto roller in casting, etc., are powered by application software.

The Enterprise Resources Planning (ERP) is an application software customized as per the requirements of the customer. It has different modules for different functions. The cost is high and the involvement of people and time is necessary. Today, the electronic commerce market has a huge potential in software market. Portals are powered by online software, which allow updating of database instantly. Those sites are running different application software.

The third category is the embedded software. The Automated Teller Machine (ATM), the metro railway ticket checking machine, the touch-screen in railway reservation, etc. are all powered by embedded software. Those software packages are built with the system and are not programmable like the general software. It is possible to change programs in these systems if required but this is not done frequently for obvious reasons.

Operating software and application software are interrelated. An application software must be compatible with the operating system. In the case of customized products, changes may have to be simultaneously made for operating and application software.

> **SPOTLIGHT**
>
> A company is manufacturing a product for the coal industry. The product is manufactured in a conveyor belt system. The conveyor belt runs with the help of an application software basically embedded in the system. The product design software is CAD, which is an engineering software. Both the software require OS to be loaded for an application software. The operator can monitor and handle the whole line of production through a control panel.

The security control and attendance system are monitored through application packages developed in-house. A readymade financial accounting package can be run in an accounts department. All machines are loaded with Windows operating system. The in-house application software is developed through "C" language. Each department has at least one office management software. The selection of programming language and software is not a general issue. One should consider factors like appropriateness, sophistication, support, efficiency and organizational constraints, etc.

Some languages are designed for special purposes, but not necessarily for the development of a suitable product in some areas. For example, FORTRAN is not suitable for business applications. Sophistication involves writing a number of codes for the development of software. For example, it may be difficult to create a table and then look up values in it unless the language has a table data structure capability. Support is important for any software, which is customized and outsourced. It is better to develop or to buy a software product that is established in the market. Although a less important feature now, the efficiency with which a language compiles and executes the program is important. The software should be easy to learn when we consider its handling by the organization. Moreover, it should be easy to maintain and change, and flexible enough so that it can help the organization grow. These organizational considerations have direct long-term cost implications.

REVIEW QUESTIONS

1. What are the major types of software?
2. How does software differ in terms of users and uses?
3. What is an operating system?
4. Describe multiprogramming, multiprocessing and time sharing.

5. Define the fourth-generation language.
6. What is application software?
7. What is the difference between system software and application software?
8. What are the advantages of customized software? What are its disadvantages?
9. What is object-oriented programming?
10. Name and discuss any office automation software.
11. What do you understand by computer language?
12. What do you understand by source code and object code?

DISCUSSION QUESTIONS

1. An organization wishes to develop a system which will be implemented for inventory management. The information department cannot perform this job alone. Comment on this statement.
2. What may drive an organization to develop its own application rather than purchase one off-the-shelf?

5

Database Management

5.1 FILE ORGANIZATION

Data are stored in the secondary storage device in the computer. Data are commonly defined as raw facts or observations, typically about any kind of transaction. Raw data can be represented in various forms or entities like voice, text and picture. The data that have been put into a meaningful and useful context to the recipient is **information**. An effective information system provides the users with timely, accurate and relevant information. The information is stored in files. Users can access these files whenever required. The computer stores data in binary form. A **bit** represents the smallest unit of data that a computer can handle. A group of 8 bits, called a **byte**, represents a single character. The character can be a number or a symbol. A grouping of characters into a **word**, a group of words or a complete number is called a **field**. A group of related fields makes up a **record**. A group of records of the same type is called **file**. A **database** is the allocation of files of the same type.

Bit	Byte	Field	Record	File	Database
0	10100001	Name			Student database
		Age			
		Year			

Figure 5.1 Data hierarchy.

    A database is the backbone of any organization. Organizations begin information processing using automatic applications in different functional areas. They develop applications in each functional area. Even within a functional area, they develop systems in isolation from other areas. Each application, of course, requires its own files and its own computer programs in order to operate. Each functional area normally shares data stored in a master file and extracts data through application programs. Data are stored in different files like master files and transaction files. Master files are the main files which normally store permanent information about entities. Records stored in the master file are related to records in transaction files. A transaction file is a collection of records describing the details of the master file. As the name suggests, a master file holds master records of any information such as bank customers or employee details of an organization. Let us discuss a case of corporate bank services. The bank has many corporate customers. A customer withdraws and deposits on daily basis. A customer may deposit twenty cheques per day. Each piece of information holds the data about the customer code, the date of deposit and the amount deposited or withdrawn. These data are stored in a transaction file, which stores day-to-day details of a customer. At the same time, the data is also stored in another file with fields like customer code, customer name, customer address, customer phone number, etc. In this case, the data is stored once, at the time of opening of a new account and there exists one record for one customer. This file is known as master file where for each record, many details are stored in the transaction file.

SPOTLIGHT

A payroll master file contains the basic information relating to salaries. The Personnel Department normally maintains this master file. The Accounts Department uses and maintains an employee's insurance file, a provident fund file, and a list of employees who joined the company up to current date. So, the two departments maintain the same type of information. On the other hand, one department copies the pertinent records and recombines the records into an intermediate file. This process leads to multiple master files which are created, maintained and operated by separate divisions and departments.

Data are stored in secondary devices for different software applications. File organization is one of the issues, which determines how the data is to be accessed. File organization is influenced by many factors such as the time to access the data from storage device, transfer data rate and modification of existing data. For small sizes of database, the speed of data transfer may not get affected but as the database size increases the speed of data transfer starts diminishing. For example, let us consider a bank database of customers in detail. There are two types of file organizations—sequential and index.

In a sequential file, the records are stored in a predetermined sequence—one after another. Sequences are determined by a particular field, technically known as the primary key. A primary key is a field as discussed in the master file which is unique in nature and therefore is used to identify that record. Primary keys are usually customer codes in a bank, student codes in a library, employee codes in a payroll, etc. Usually, the records are stored on tapes in ascending order in the sequential file. In a sequential file, the records are processed sequentially, that is, when using a sequential access to reach a particular record, all the records preceding it must be processed first. This means that to read a record stored at the end of the file, each of the records preceding must be processed first. The process is slow in nature. But sequential processing at a particular interval like monthly bill calculation, payroll calculation is very efficient and cost effective, as magnetic tapes are used as media. The efficiency of a sequential file depends on the types of query used to manipulate data. In case of a query involving multiple selection of records other than the primary keys, they are processed by reading the entire file to find the matching criteria. The process of manipulation of data such as update, inserting a new record, etc. are complex. The reason is that the new record can neither be updated nor be removed in a sequential file.

In direct file processing, unlike sequential file processing, the data are organized to support direct access throughout the disk. It is possible to access any record instantaneously and in any order. The record can be updated any time and the system can respond to another query once the earlier process is complete. This is nothing but an online transaction processing system. In direct access processing, the system does not search the entire file, rather it moves directly to the record. In an index file, a primary index is created, which associates the primary key with the physical location in which a record is stored. The primary index file contains two pieces of information, the record key and the physical address of the record. When a user seeks a record, the operating application software first loads the primary index into the computer's CPU and then searches the index sequentially for the key. It finds the address and reads the record associated with this address. Even though indexing is a two-step process, it is more efficient than a sequential search in which a user has to start looking from the beginning of the record and continue till the required object is found. It is possible to manipulate data for a difficult type of query in an index file, as the primary index file locates the address faster for processing records.

Index sequential is another method of file organization which combines the features of both sequential and direct access. In index sequential, a secondary index file is created in addition to primary index in which all the records are arranged by ascending and descending order of the primary key. In this way, the file structure of the organization becomes so complex that the situation results in growing inefficiency and complexity. Over the years, the organization will be saddled with hundreds of programs, data files, and inefficient people who would not know what to do, what data to use and who else is using the data. The results are data redundancy, poor data security, and inconsistency.

5.2 DATABASE MANAGEMENT

Data redundancy occurs when duplicate data are stored in multiple data files. Generally, in an organization, different functional areas or divisions independently collect the same piece of information.

> **SPOTLIGHT**
>
> The Accounts Department stores information of sundry debtors and the same data is also maintained by the stores. The Accounts Department uses this information to manage debtors as well as working capital whereas the Stores Department uses the same information for challan and invoice management. Those data used by a programmer have different meanings and the analyst works in isolation on various applications.

Programs are data dependent. Programs manipulate data and prepare the report based on the user's requirements. Data updating and maintenance are very important to the users. In traditional file environment, any change in the data, requires to change all the areas where the data is stored. Such changes cost substantial amount of money and time. Program-data dependency is another aspect in this area.

Business needs ad hoc data or reports of unanticipated situations. But a traditional file environment can deliver only routine schedule reports but not adorable reports. Several programs would have to work together to develop a report as required by the user. So this system is not flexible enough to maintain.

Security is one of the major aspects in any information system. In the traditional information system, there is very little control over data, and dissemination of information is virtually not possible. As a result, it becomes difficult to find information in many cases as required by the user. Data sharing is not possible because pieces of information lie in different files and different parts of the organization. The traditional information system, thus, lacks the qualities of sharing and availability of information.

The above problems, inherent in the traditional file system, can be solved using database technology. A **database** is a collection of data organized to serve many applications and operations by centralizing the data. Data are stored in a centralized location rather than in separate files. A single database serves multiple applications.

A **Database Management System (DBMS)** is a collection of programs that enables the organization to store, manipulate and manage data efficiently. DBMS is the interface between the database and the application programs. DBMS consists of three components as follows:

- A data definition language
- A data manipulation language
- A data dictionary

The data definition language is the formal language used by programmers to specify the content and structure of the database. It defines data elements as they appear in the database.

Most of the database management systems are based on data manipulation language that is used in conjunction with some conventional languages. The languages help to extract data from the database to satisfy information requests and the development of applications. Structured Query Language (SQL) is the standard data manipulation language for a relational database management system.

The third component of a database management system is a data dictionary. It stores definitions of data elements and data characteristics such as usage, physical representation, etc. It stores all the data definitions used in the system and serves as an important data management tool.

The following discussion illustrates the advantages of database management systems:

- The centrally managed data reduces the complexity of the organization's information system for access, utilization and security.
- Data redundancy and consistency can be reduced by eliminating all the isolated files, where the same data exists
- Program development and maintenance costs can be reduced to manage data centrally.
- Access and availability of information can be increased.

5.3 DATABASE DESIGN

Data can be related in alternative ways in a database. Conventional database management systems use one of the three principal logical database models. They are as follows:

- Hierarchical database model
- Network database model
- Relational database model
- Object-oriented model

Each logical model has certain advantages in the context of business and processing purpose.

Hierarchical database model

The earliest database management system was **hierarchical**, and one of the oldest database models. In this model, the relationship is represented by a tree structure. It represents the relationship in the same way as an organizational hierarchy is defined. The most common hierarchical database management system is the IBM's Information Management System (IMS). It was developed jointly by North American Rockwell Company and IBM. IMS became one of the leading mainframe hierarchical database models in 1970s and early 1980s. In this model, the data elements are organized into pieces of records called segments. It looks like an organizational chart with one top-level segment called the root. An upper segment is connected logically to a lower segment in a parent–child relationship. A child can have only one parent but a parent can have more than one child.

Figure 5.2 shows a hierarchical model structure similar to the one used

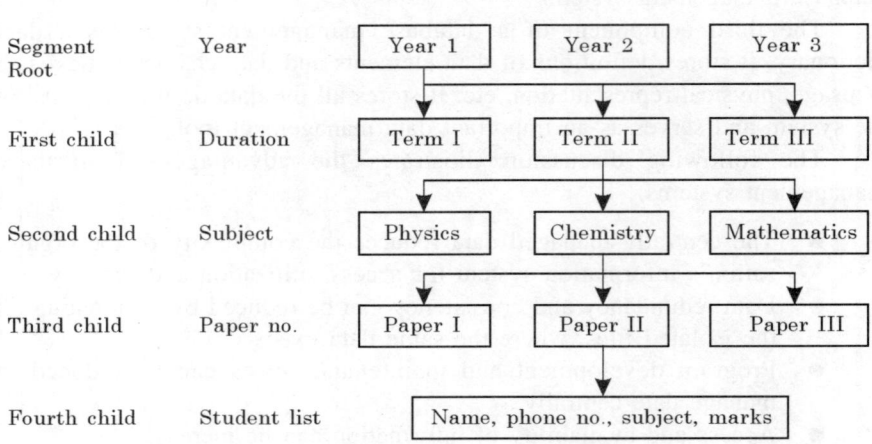

Figure 5.2 Hierarchical database model.

in a college. Root is the year of the study. In the college, a student is admitted for three years and each year consists of a trimester. Each trimester has subjects with different papers. In a hierarchical database management system, the data are physically linked to another by a series of pointers that form chains of related data segments. Pointers are data elements attached to the ends of record segments on the disk directing the system to related records. In our example, the end of year segment would contain a series of pointers to all the possible directions. In turn, at the end of the duration segment, there are pointers to the subjects belong to that trimester.

In this model, the relationship between the various segments are logically simple, so the design is not complex. It was the first model that offered data security. The parent–child relationship enforces good level of integrity. In one-to-many relationships, this model works efficiently.

Although a hierarchical database model is simple to understand but it has **disadvantages** too. Any change in the database structure requires a change in all the application programs; hence time and cost are the important issues to consider. The pointer concept, as discussed, requires knowledge of complex pointer system, which is often an obstacle to the user. Also, many of the relationships of data are not the common ones, for example, 1:n (one to many) that may be required by the model. The many-to-many relationships are very difficult to implement in this model.

Network database model

The network database model is the logical database model based on many-to-many relationships. Database can be translated from hierarchical to network and vice versa in consideration with the processing speed and convenience. For example, the data in Figure 5.3 can be represented by a hierarchical

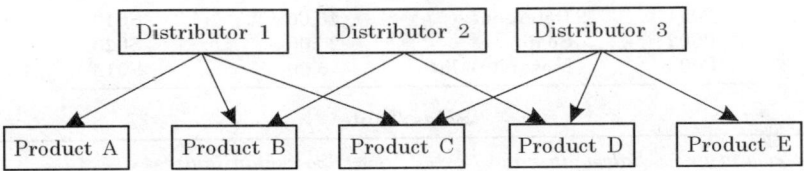

Figure 5.3 Network database model.

model but it creates considerable redundancy and a slow response to certain types of information queries. Those kinds of problems are sorted out by a network database model. The number of pointers in the network database model, however, increases rapidly, making maintenance and operations more expensive. The network database model supports both one-to-many and many-to-many relationships. Data independence is another benefit of this model, i.e. up to a certain extent the changes in the data characteristics do not require changes in the programs.

The major **disadvantage** of the network database model is that all of the access paths, directories and indices must be specified in advance. It is not possible to change them easily without a major programming effort.

Both hierarchical database model and network database model have their own advantages and disadvantages. Both of these models have now been replaced by the relational database model.

Relational database model

The relational database model represents all the data in the database as simple two-dimensional tables called *relations*. Figure 5.4 shows a sales table, a product table and a stock table. In each table, the rows contain records and the columns contain fields. The term table is used as row or record in the relational table. Each table has one common data element with the other. Herein lies the strength of the relational database model. Any table can share any data with another table as long as both tables share a common data element. For example, suppose we wanted to find the name and the address of the salesperson who could sell the products P001 and P003, we would then need information from two tables: from the Sales table and from the Product table. Note that these two tables have a shared data element: Salesman number.

Stock Table

Order no.	Date	Product no.
0120	22/07/02	P001
0121	25/07/02	P002

Product Table

Product no.	Description	Price	Salesman no.
P001	Detergent	45.00	S013
P002	Soap	26.00	S026
P003	Mosquito Mat	5.00	S013

Sales Table

Salesman no.	Salesman name	Salesman address
S011	Jayanta	Deshbandhunagar, Baguati, Kolkata-700059
S013	Farida	43, Ratan Babu Road, Kolkata-700002.
S013	Antony	125, Neogi Para Road, Kolkata-700036.

Figure 5.4 Relational database model.

The basic operations used in a relational database model are as follows:

- Select
- Joint
- Project

Select creates records to meet certain criteria. The Joint combines relational tables to provide the user with more information than an individual table can provide. The Project extracts data from part of the table or tables as required by the user. The **strength** of the relational database model lies in its flexibility with regard to any queries. It has the power to combine information from different sources, coupled with the added attraction of simplicity of design and maintenance. It is easy to add new data and records without disturbing the programs and the applications.

The **weakness** of the relational database model is its low processing capability. The system is slower because it requires many accesses to the data store on the disk to carry out selects, joints and project commands.

Object-oriented model

The major objective of object-oriented model is to eliminate the flaws encountered in other database models. Object-oriented programming attempts to eliminate some pitfalls of conventional programming. It incorporates the best structured programming with several new approaches. It is a new approach to develop programs and has nothing to do with any particular language. Generally, not all languages are suitable to implement the object-oriented concept (OOC). Smalltalk, C++, Ada and Java are the languages that support OOC. Java is a true object-oriented language. It ties data more closely to the functions that operates on it and protects it from unintentional modification by other functions. In this model, it allows decomposing a problem into a number of entities called objects and then build data and functions around these entities. An object is a combination of data and functions. Here emphasis is on data rather than on procedure. Programs are divided into objects and new data and methods can be easily added whenever necessary.

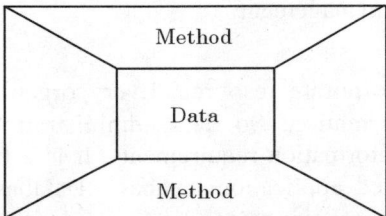

Figure 5.5 Object = Data + Method.

An object may represent a person, a place, a bank account, a table of data or any other item that the program can handle. Objects may also represent user defined data types. The benefits of object-oriented database is that we can build programs from the standard working modules that communicate with one another. This helps to save cost and time. It is easy to make partitions of the work in a project, based on objects. An object-oriented system can be easily upgraded from a small to a large system. Software complexity in an object-oriented system can be easily managed.

Object-oriented languages often offer many benefits to the program designers. They offer productivity with quality software and low maintenance costs. One can develop programs from standard modules rather than writing new codes. This leads to saving of time. The object-oriented technology is continuously under development and current products do get superseded quickly.

5.4 MANAGEMENT AND DATABASE

The database is an organizational discipline, a method, rather than a tool or technology. It faces challenges in the organization. Management support is an important part for database development. The elements in a database management system are as follows (Figure 5.6):

1. Database administration
2. Database management

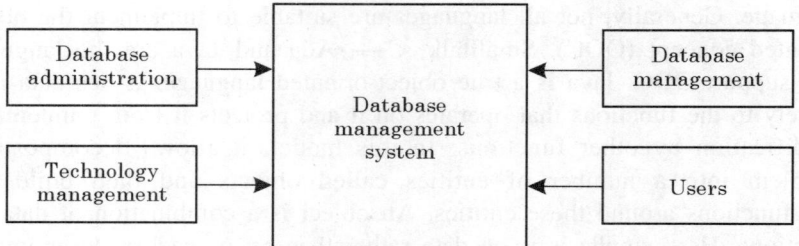

Figure 5.6 Management and database.

3. Technology management
4. Users

Database is a corporate resource. Every organization recognizes the strategic role of information. So data administration is a function with the power to define information requirements. It is a function to address the problem of unintegrated application database. Database administration in a large organization may require many database administrators. In such cases, there is a group of database administrators who share the responsibility. A database administrator's responsibilities are:

- Installation, upgradation, development of the database and applications tools.
- Storage system management for the present situation and to meet the future requirements.
- User management such as controlling and monitoring the access of the database, authorization of user, etc.
- Planning for database backup and recovery.
- Helping the user and coordinating with the software vendors.

As such, a data administrator develops the data model, the data standards, and eliminates unnecessary data redundancy and data access methods. Data administration must evolve into data management in the true term. An organization requires formulating information management and planning policy that specifies its rules for sharing, acquiring, classifying and standardization. A database management system serves a broader role than a traditional file environment. Enterprise planning and management is a major part, which addresses the information requirements.

New technology is another aspect of database management system. It plays a vital role in achieving competitive advantage. Technology adaptation through-out the organization is not an easy process. The management has to be focused and ready to accept the changes. The organization must have long-term strategy to implement technology challenges. It is not possible to buy new hardware to implement new technology every year. So, the management is required to focus on future aspects of the technology as well.

Another way, the information system department must take part in formulating strategy. So, training of staff and adequate technology development are the points to be considered.

In today's context, managements are more concerned with database management tools and techniques. Data are distributed throughout the organization. It is not only just the factory or the head office, but at the same time data is made accessible to the suppliers, dealers, etc. The customer database is huge in size, not restricted to one region only, but spread throughout the world. Information enquires demand extraction from distributed sources to support decision-making tasks. Senior-level executives do not need operational and transaction level information to support their decision-making activities. They normally require summarized information at different points of time. Data information is available with different departments in a large organization. Different departments design their operational database based on available resources and requirements. They also maintain a large database from heterogeneous, multiple and distributed sources. The integration of data desirable from the point of view of top-level management.

A **data warehouse** is such an integrated collection of data that supports decision-making processes. In a broader sense, a data warehouse uses the tools to store summarized information from multiple heterogeneous databases into a single repository. It is not just operational data. Multiple databases are stored in a summarized form in a data warehouse. **Data warehousing** is a process of integrating heterogeneous databases into a single place. A data warehouse is therefore not a database in the traditional concept.

The concept of a data warehouse is based on the multidimensional data model. This model views data in the form of a data cube. In a three-dimensional architecture, all the three dimensions represent data. For example, for an employee the three dimensions may be sex, profession and year. After building a data warehouse, the next step is to explore analytical tools to perform analysis. These data analysis tools are called On Line Analytical Processing (OLAP).

It is not possible to find out the pattern of customers' buying habits by general query languages. There are data mining techniques which support automatic exploration. Data mining can identify the patterns and trends in the data. Those developments have provided new possibilities for exploration of a data warehouse. This is a new approach to enterprise-wide computing. It is nothing but a competitive tool available to the organization.

Users are not only those who deal with the end product, but also programmers and specialists. Professional system workers must be available in a database management system. The implementation of a database requires widespread changes in the organization including defining the role of database and allocation of power at senior levels.

> **SPOTLIGHT**
>
> An organization maintains an attendance system in a computerized information processing system. An attendance card, which is a plastic magnetic card, is issued to each employee. The card reader is placed at the entrance point of the office. Each employee has to punch the card at the time of entry and exit. The card reader is linked with the computer of the Human Resource (HR) department. The computer is loaded with a software, which manages the attendance database. The card reader can store data for one week. Once the card reader is full, it cannot read the card. The software that manages the database cannot recognize the problem. The computer operator in HR department is also not aware of this problem. So, once the card shows an error, he informs the distributor for rectifying the problem. The product needs to be replaced at that juncture.

The costs of transformation from one platform to other database environment are tangible, upfront and large in the long run. Many organizations avoid those commitments and organizational changes in the short run. Eventually, this results in an incompatible database that fails to address the key issues in the organization.

REVIEW QUESTIONS

1. What is file management?
2. Define a database and Database Management System (DBMS).
3. List some of the benefits of having a Database Management System.
4. Describe three principal Database Management System models, and the advantages and disadvantages of each model.
5. What is an object-oriented model?
6. What is an object-oriented database?
7. What are the differences between the traditional file management and data management?
8. Name and describe the three components of a Database Management System.

DISCUSSION QUESTIONS

1. Database design is the most important part of the Database Management System. Comment on this statement.
2. Which industries are most dependent on the operation of large databases?
3. Discuss the current database trend.

6

Business Data Communication

6.1 DATA COMMUNICATION AND NETWORK

Data communication is the transmission of data, from one point to another, between two devices, say, from one computer to another computer. Data communication between two remote devices can be achieved through computer networks. A computer network is a system wherein the computer communicates with other 'intelligent devices' such as printers, scanners, etc. In a desktop standalone computer system, data is shared only through a removable storage device, such as a CD, pendrive, etc. Here each desktop system consists of its own printer, modem, and scanner and cannot communicate with another computer. On the other hand, in a network system, computer resources are shared within a group of computers connected under the same network. In the most basic sense, such a computer network system allows any kind of digital information—numerical data, text, pictures, voice, and video—to be exchanged among different types of communicating devices. A computer network, therefore, enables a company to extend the size and scope of its business operations, thus enhancing interpersonal communications among staff and providing direct links to customers and business associates for easy exchange of information. Some common examples of computer networks are discussed in this chapter.

Telephone systems are the most common kind of networks used for data communication. Business houses and organizations use their own Private Branch Exchange (PBX). Telephone companies service their customers through larger networks. Facsimile transmission involves the same type of communication processing. The terminal is a fax machine capable of scanning, transmitting, and printing documents.

Electronic mail allows a user to send and receive mails to anywhere and anytime. A user composes a message or can attach a previously created document, picture, voice to the receiver, and it stores messages, so the receiver need not be working on the computer at the time that the e-mail is received. Electronic data interchange, which has revolutionized the banking and financial services, enables transfer of funds between two accounts. An Automated Teller Machines (ATM) is a visible example of electronic funds transfer in the banking industry.

In an organization, several computers are connected together through a network system. An employee can access information available in any of those computers, sitting at his workplace. At the same time, he can use all other common resources like printers, scanners, files, etc. Electronic commerce has dramatically changed the way the firms do business. It has contributed to serving customers in a much better way than was possible earlier. Business houses can communicate throughout the world, incurring a very low cost. The cost of communication has come down rapidly, enabling the companies to reap the benefits of modern technology for improving their performance. This is nothing but the application of Internet in the industry. Many commercial enterprises are now exploring how the Internet and other kinds of interorganizational systems can create new kinds of electronic markets, enabling the distribution of business information in entirely new ways. In network architecture, **client/server** computing is a popular model because it offers several benefits. The main feature of client/server is that it contains co-operative programming capabilities. The process or a set of processes resides on the server. The client has processing capabilities and makes requests to server, via Local Area Network (LAN). The client, the server and the network form the client/server architecture. The user gets the feeling of his direct involvement with software, data and hardware, and the system. At the workstations or nodes, the user can manipulate data and execute the programs received from the server. Client/server is connected via different media—conducted or radiated. Client or workstation is connected with the server by a different topology. It also requires other hardware devices to communicate with the client/server architecture.

6.2 COMMUNICATION MEDIA

The characteristics of a communication medium comprise the speed of transmission, the direction in which signals may travel and the mode of transmission. The unit of measurement of information that can be transmitted through any telecommunication channel is bits per second (bps). Sometimes this is referred to as band rate. A band is a binary event representing a signal change from positive to negative. One signal change, or cycle, is required to transmit one or several bits per second (bps); the transmission capacity depends on frequency. Frequency, in data communications, refers to the number of times per second that a current passes through a complete cycle. The measure of frequency is hertz (Hz), which represents one cycle per second. The communication time in a network depends on the medium, and its capacity to carry information is known as **bandwidth**. Bandwidth is a range of frequencies, stated in terms of hertz (Hz). The bandwidth refers to how much data carrying capacity is available on the line.

Information flows in the form of electromagnetic signals. There are two types of signals—analog and digital. An analog signal is a continuous waveform that passes through a communication medium. A digital signal, on the other hand, is a discrete form of signal rather than a continuous waveform. It transmits data in two discrete states often as 1s and 0s, which are represented as on-off electrical pulses. There are several conventions for transmitting signals. A convention is necessary when a character begins or ends. Synchronous transmission transmits one character at a time at a low speed. In a synchronous transmission, large volume of data is transmitted at high speeds. Another characteristic deals with the direction of data flow over a telecommunication network. In simplex transmission, data can travel only in one direction at all times. In half-duplex transmission, data can flow two ways but can travel in only one direction at a time. In full-duplex transmission, the data can be sent in both directions simultaneously.

A network system cannot exist without a medium to connect the source and the receiver. The medium provides a path through which messages are sent. The media can be of two types: one that is visible like the physical wire or cable and the other is wireless transmission. The former medium is known as *conducted* and the latter as *radiated*. A channel can utilize different kinds of communication transmission media—twisted pair wire, coaxial cable, fibre optic cable, terrestrial microwave, cellular and satellite.

Twisted Pair Wire

The most common transmission medium in use is the twisted pair wire Twisted pair, the least expensive physical medium, consists of two copper wires twisted together. The common example is the telephone system in a building for the transmission of voice (analog) signals. Twisted pair wire is available in two types: Shielded Twisted Pair (STP) and Unshielded Twisted Pair (UTP). In STP, a twisted pair of copper conductors each with its own plastic insulation, is placed into a metallic shield, which is a wrapping made of thin wires to absorb any interference, and finally the shielded pair put into a plastic outer shell (Figure 6.1). On the other hand, UTP wire does not have the wire wrapping like that of the STP wire. It is adequate for voice transmission. The capacity of the twisted pair wire is up to 10 megabytes per second (MBPS), which is adequate for connecting microcomputers and other office devices. One drawback of the twisted pair wire is that it emits

Figure 6.1 Twisted pair cable.

electromagnetic radiation creating interference in the signal transmission. The signal degrades over a long distance and requires amplifiers.

Coaxial Cable

Another widely used data communication medium is coaxial cable, which consists of a central core conductor of solid or stranded wire (usually copper) enclosed in an insulating sheath, which, in turn, is encased in an outer conductor of metal foil, braid, or a combination of both. The outer metallic wrapping serves both as a shield against interference and as the second conductor which completes the circuit. This outer shield is also enclosed in an insulating sheath and whole cable is protected by a plastic cover (Figure 6.2). The coaxial cable is used for applications requiring higher

Figure 6.2 Coaxial cable.

performance than a twisted pair cable can provide. The coaxial cable, often called *coax*, is a high bandwidth medium that can carry thousands of signals at once. The shield protects the core conductor and, therefore, the signal creates a path that is more resistant to electrical interference and noise. It helps to reduce the chances of errors being introduced into the signal and enables larger amounts of data to travel through the cable. Coaxial cable allows for two types of transmissions. The cable television industry makes use of broadband transmission, in which a single cable is divided electrically into many channels, each carrying a different transmission. Broadband transmission is analog. The second type of transmission used with coaxial cable is the baseband transmission. It is a digital transmission and only one signal is transmitted over the cable. It requires specialized wiring. The coaxial cable signals degrade over long distances and require amplifiers. Another drawback of the coaxial cable is that it is much larger and heavier than the twisted pair cable.

Fibre Optic Cable

Fibre optic cables are small strands of glass or plastic that carry signals in the form of light, rather than electrical signals. The light transmits digital signals by using pulses of light to represent 0s and 1s. Fibres of glass or plastic can transmit large amount of information over long distances and are resistant to electrical interference providing very 'clear', error-free transmission. Theoretically, a single pair of fibre optic cable can transmit ten terabits of information per second. Fibre optic cable is considerably faster, more durable and lighter than the wire media and well suited for the transfer of large volume of data. On the other side, fibre optic cable is expensive and more difficult to work with and requires a complex installation process. High-speed fibre optic cables have many advantages. In addition to speed, security is also more in the case of fibre optic cables. Another advantage is the immunity of the fibre optic cable to electrical interference which causes crosstalk in the case of copper wire. Fibre optic cable is almost used exclusively as the backbone of a network connection, while twisted wire and coaxial cable are used to connect the last legs to reach consumers at their homes and offices on their desktops.

Wireless Transmission

Wireless transmission sends signals through air or space, which medium does not require any physical connection. The electromagnetic waves can be broadcast efficiently through an antenna of appropriate size. Wireless communication is based on this principle. All electromagnetic waves travel at the same speed in vacuum. This speed does not depend on frequency. This speed, c, is approximately 3×10^8 m/s, usually called the speed of light.

The number of oscillations per second of an electromagnetic wave is called its frequency, f. The distance between two consecutive maxima or minima is called wavelength and is denoted by λ. The fundamental relation between f, λ and c is

$$\lambda f = c \text{ [in vacuum]}$$

The speed of light, c, is constant, so if the value of λ is available, we can find f and vice versa. The radio, microwaves, infrared and visible light portion of the spectrum are used for transmitting information. The transmission is better on higher frequencies. Through ultraviolet light, X-rays and gamma rays would be better due to their higher frequencies but these rays are injurious to the health of living things. The amount of information that an electro-magnetic wave can carry is related to its bandwidth.

Radio waves can travel over a long distance and propagate well through buildings. Radio waves are also easy to generate, so they are widely used. Radio waves can travel in all directions from its source, thus the transmitter and receiver can be aligned in any direction. These waves are frequency dependent, absorbed by rain. The low frequency (LF) and medium frequency (MF), radio waves propagate along the ground.

The forms of transmission that use radiated media are terrestrial microwaves, satellites, cellular telephones or infrared light rays. Terrestrial microwave systems transmit higher-frequency signals (3000 MHZ to 30 GHZ) between stations. This is a widely used, long-distant, point-to-point communication. Terrestrial microwave uses a fixed transmitting antenna to focus a narrow beam and provide the 'line-of-sight' transmission to a fixed receiving antenna. Microwave signals travel in straight lines and do not bend with the curvature of the earth. Microwave signals can get degraded by rain and snow and by obstacles between microwave stations. Normally, microwave antennas are, therefore, usually located on hills or tall buildings, so that they can transmit over the straight path, without any obstacles. In highly congested areas, the effectiveness of this transmission decreases.

Satellites are used typically in the large geographically dispersed organization that would be difficult to communicate through cables and microwave transmission. Satellites are on geosynchronous rotations, 22,300 miles above the equator; provide data and telecommunications to remote areas. The gravity of the earth keeps the satellite revolving in orbit at the same rate as that of the earth's rotation (a geosynchronous orbit); thus, the satellite appears to be in a fixed position above the earth. It also serves as a back up to office fibre cables and microwave communications. Such satellites are called Geosynchronous Earth Orbiting Satellites (GEOSs). The signal from a satellite can reach only a certain part of the earth called footprint, which generally covers several countries. Only the earth stations within the footprint of the satellite can receive the transmission of such a satellite. Three satellites positioned around the equator can transmit signals over the entire earth. Over the last few years, many business houses in India have connected their far-flung offices, warehouses through network using Very Small Apparatus Terminals (VSATs)—small, low-cost satellite dishes that economically transmits voice, data and video communication. National Stock Exchange branches are connected through a VSATs system throughout India. New types of satellites are gaining popularity, such as Low Earth Orbiting Satellites (LEOSs), which orbit the earth at a height of 325 to 1000 miles. Medium Earth Orbiting Satellites (MEOSs) are similar to Low Earth Orbiting Satellites (LEOSs), except that they are positioned at 6000 to 10,000 miles above the earth.

Cellular telephones (also called mobile telephones) are radio devices that use cellular radio signals to transmit voice and messages. The radio antennas are placed within adjacent geographic areas called cells. The transmitters in adjacent cells can broadcast on the same frequency and not interfere with one another. The emerging technologies can provide high-speed networks over a wide area, making cellular devices much more cost effective.

Many factors are involved in selecting a media for network communication. The cost of replacing existing media is also important. Four factors are considered for selecting the media—cost, speed, rate of error and security.

Infrared waves are widely used for short-range communication. The remote controls used for televisions, VCRs and stereos are based on infrared communication. Infrared waves are relatively omni directional, cheap and easy to build, but cannot pass through solid objects. Infrared systems do not interfere with other similar systems. No licence is required to operate the infrared systems.

Cost factors not only include the medium itself but also include the distance between two computers. The least expensive medium for data communication is untwisted shielded pair wire cable. It is also inexpensive to add with another network. Coaxial cable is more expensive than the twisted pair and it depends on the cable used. Fibre optic cable is the most expensive. Satellite channel costs are based on distance and the speed of the transmission. The speed of the communication has been improving with the technology and media type. The oldest medium category (category 1 UTP) is the slowest. Next comes the coaxial cable, terrestrial microwaves and satellite microwaves. Finally, the highest speed available is with the fibre optic. One of the biggest factors to be considered in data communication is the reduction or the elimination of errors. Most transmission errors come from a distortion of the signal through communication channels. This distortion reduces the strength of the signal. Twisted pair wire and coaxial cable are prone to interference produced by magnets. Terrestrial and satellite microwave transmission can be interrupted by weather.

Security from stealing data is needed. For example, it is easy to tap twisted pair and coaxial cable because they are made of copper. Fibre optic cable is harder to be tapped and security problem and breaches are easily detected. Broadcast transmission (satellites, terrestrial microwave) is of low security. The data is transmitted through air and anyone with an antenna or a satellite dish can intercept the data.

6.3 NETWORK TOPOLOGY

Networks can be configured in different ways to organize communication with the help of equipment connected together through links. The term topology is used to refer to the way in which a network is laid out physically. Distance and bandwidth are the major determinants of network topologies. Networks can also be classified by their topology or shape as well as by their geographic scope and type of service they provide. While a Local Area Network (LAN) links local resources in the same department and building of a firm, a Wide Area Network (WAN) encompasses a relatively wide geographic area. The three most common topologies used are as follows:

- Star
- Bus
- Ring

Star topology: A star network is a network configuration in which all of the PCs, printers and other devices on the network are connected to a central system. The design concept is based on use of a centralized mainframe computing system, where terminals (PCs) and other resources are connected to a mainframe host computer (Figure 6.3). This topology is useful for applications where part of the processing is centralized and some can be processed locally.

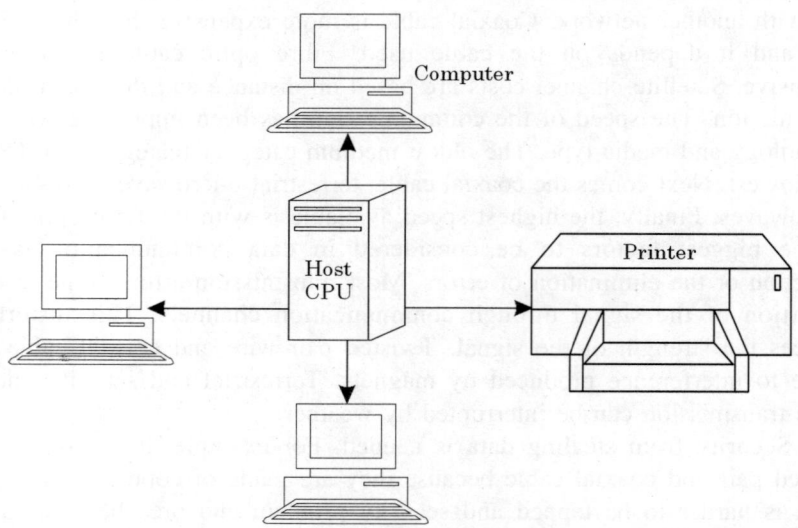

Figure 6.3 Star topology.

Star topology is also useful when system management most appropriately resides at a single point. Here point-to-point communication lines connect the central system with other physical devices like PCs, printers, etc. The central system serves as a communication switch, explicitly directing the flow of information from any one device; through the network, to its destination. In a star network, all communications are therefore managed from a central printer or central computer. The main problem is that the communication in the network will come to a standstill if the host computer stops functioning. Alternative topologies enable multiple devices to interconnect with one another, without necessarily causing a single point failure.

Bus topology: A bus topology provides a central communication channel connecting multiple devices to a single circuit made of twisted wire cable or coaxial cable or fibre optic cable (Figure 6.4). All the signals are broadcast through the bus cable. The network software identifies which devices receive messages. There is no central host system; the failure of any individual computer does not necessarily affect the rest of the network.

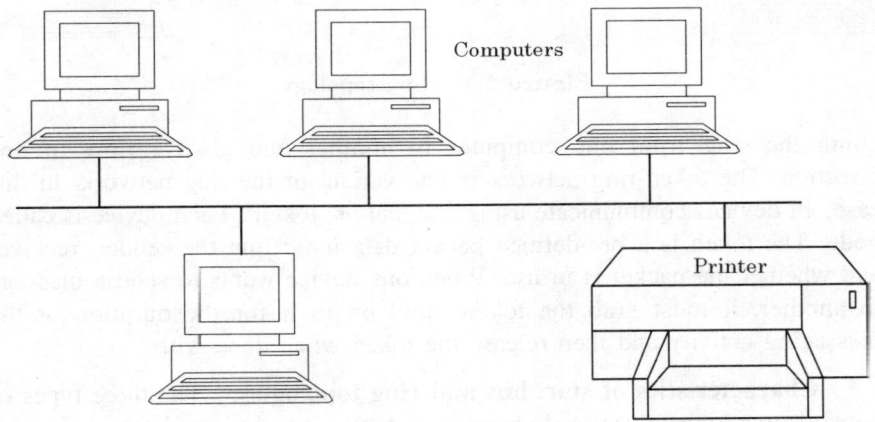

Figure 6.4 Bus topology.

The ends of the bus cable have a special device connected to them called the *terminator*, telling the network the end locations. Since the bus network is dependent upon a single wire, whenever any problem occurs in the wire, the entire network goes down. However if a single station or terminal on the network fails, the network can continue to operate as long as the other network devices are operational.

Ring topology: A ring topology is the third kind of networking configuration. Like the bus network topology, the ring network topology does not also depend on any host computer and will not necessarily break down when any one computer or terminal malfunctions. Each computer can communicate with each other and also can process information independently.

The ring topology is designed such that each workstation is connected to another workstation before it and to a second workstation after it. The connecting cables form a closed loop or ring (Figure 6.5). Data are processed

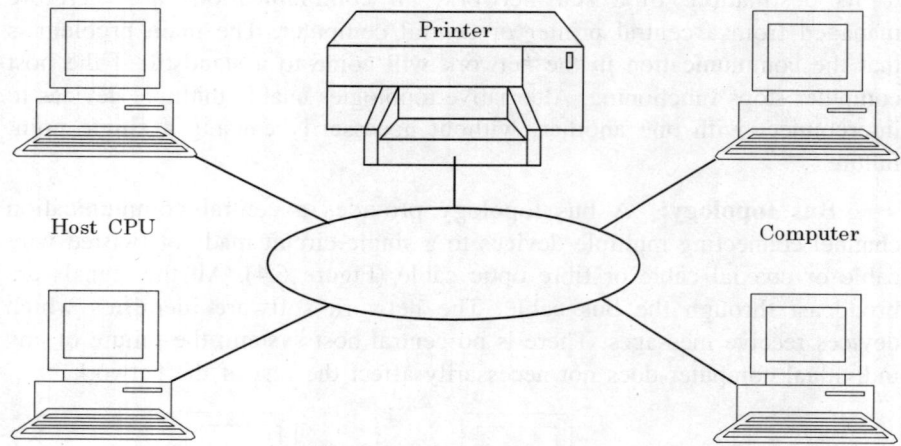

Figure 6.5 Ring topology.

along the ring from one computer to another and always flow in one direction. The token-ring network is one variant of the ring network. In this case, all devices communicate using a signal or 'token'. Each device is called node. The token is a pre-defined packet data indicating the sender, receiver and whether the packet is in use. When one device wants to send a message to another, it must grab the token, hold on to it for the duration of the messaging activity and then release the token when done with.

Characteristics of star, bus and ring topologies: The three types of network topologies discussed above have their own characteristics. It is very easy to implement the star network, because there is only one terminal on each line. Addition and deletion of terminals to or from the network can be made easily without any major changes to the network.

The difference between a bus network topology and a ring network topology is that, in a bus network, the ends of the cables are not connected to any device but are terminated in component called terminator. The bus network is inexpensive and easy to install. One advantage is that the server on the network can be attached at any point along the cable. Each workstation is connected to the bus using a short cable called drop line, which reduces the cost of the network.

6.4 NETWORK CLASSIFICATIONS

As discussed earlier, networks can be classified in different ways. Typical classifications are by geographic scope and network ownership. A network that geographically connects those who are in the same office, building, or within the same campus, is called the Local Area Network (LAN).

> **SPOTLIGHT**
>
> In an office, the LAN interconnects PCs, printers and electronic files, and allows people to share all peripherals. In an educational institutional set-up, faculty members sit in different rooms. The server is located in a separate room. A high quality laser printer is available in the printing room. A software installed in the server allows the users to access the printer. The software can also keep track of the number of copies printed by each user. Any faculty can access any file from any other computer, can take printout through the common printer and can also restrict access to other users. Each user in the LAN can share all devices connected to this network.

Typically, LAN allows to send a large amount of data over relatively short distances. It is possible to send 10 megabytes per second (MBPS) data over a distance of 1000 to 2000 metres. Individual LANs can be further interconnected with specialized hardware devices known as bridges to create a more extensive 'campus-wide' LAN.

Networks that connect distant locations—linking cities or countries around the world—are called Wide Area Networks (WANs). A network spanning a single organization or enterprise is known as enterprise network. Typically in a WAN, data can be transmitted at the speed of 56 kilobytes per second (KBPS) to 1.5 megabytes per second. Networks that connect multiple organizations are known as **inter-organizational networks**.

Networks are also classified as public networks and private networks. Generally public networks are hardware and software communication systems provided by companies. These networks are licensed and regulated by government. The standard telephone line at a home is a public line. This line primarily handles voice communications but can also be used for data communication through a modem. Public lines can be dial-up lines and leased lines.

A local network may consist of a PBX and a LAN. A PBX (Private Branch Exchange) is a central switch in a company's telephone system. This system connects all the telephone lines in the organization by three to four digit numbers. Today's PBX can carry voice and data to create local networks. They can store, transfer, hold and redial telephone calls through this network. The **advantages** of this PBX are that they utilize the existing telephone system and do not require special wiring. The PBX is supported by commercial vendors; an organization does not require any expertise to manage it. The geographic scope of PBX is limited, usually only several hundred feet. The **disadvantage** of a **PBX system** (Figure 6.6) is that it is connected through telephone lines and they cannot handle large volume of data easily.

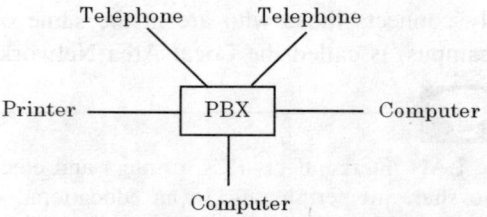

Figure 6.6 A PBX system.

A LAN encompasses a short distance, normally one building or could be several buildings in close proximity. A LAN is widely used to connect personal computers. We will discuss the server-based LAN system, which is mostly used in organizations all over the world (Figure 6.7). In this type of

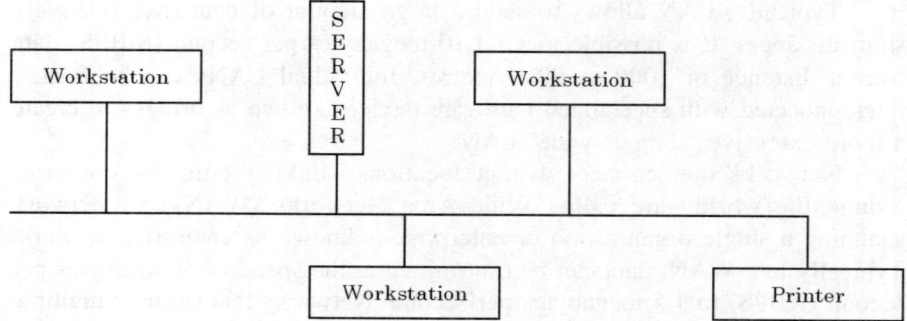

Figure 6.7 Server-based Local Area Network.

Local Area Network, software and files are stored on one or more hard disks in a central computer and all other computers on the network can access those files and data. The computer or computers shared by other computers is thus known as server or file server. LAN allows an organization to share expensive hardware and software. A colour laserjet printer is a very expensive piece of equipment. It can be shared by all the computers connected to the network.

In a Local Area Network, all users can access the same software loaded in the server. For example, in an accounting software, the user can input data from any computer of the network and the output data are stored in the central computer, where the software is loaded. So, the task of updating a software with a new version is made simpler because all software packages are loaded on a single computer instead of installing them individually on each computer.

The network version of software is used, permitting a specific number of users to access this software. The software pack comes with a 5-users' or 10-users' version, where the user specifies the number of computers or users that need to work simultaneously. A user can access any file or data from another computer without disturbing any other user. In addition, Local Area Network users have the ability to store files on the server so that such files can be accessed by other users on the LAN. The access facility is normally controlled by network software. The person responsible for installing and maintaining LAN is known as the **System Administrator**.

The file server stores various programs and data files for network program users. The server basically contains the LANs operating system, which manages the server and thus routes and manages communication on the network.

A database server is used to maintain any huge database on the network. A server which holds information about the credit card holders is an example of a database server. A user performs the necessary query, searches for data and sends only the actual record requested. The traffic on the network is reduced by processing data in the server. This server usually is a different computer than the normal network file server.

LANs are thus made of computers, cables, network cards, operating systems and application software. The communication between computers is possible, when all those are commissioned properly. The cables and network cards are vendor specific and relatively easy to install. The network operating system is used to run the network. The server is loaded with the network operating system, which takes over most of the functions of the operating system as long as the network is active. Other computers in the network are loaded with operating systems compatible with the network operating system. WINDOWS operating systems work independently of any operating system. Novell Netware is used with DOS. LINUX is a fast growing operating system that has applications in networks as well can be used on desktops.

A Wide Area Network (WAN) consists of a server and several clients (clients are all other computers other than the server) that are located in a widely dispersed geographical area (Figure 6.8). A Kolkata-based company may have branch offices in Delhi and Mumbai. In order to connect all the three locations, a WAN is needed. A network of this type usually uses dial-up or leased communication lines. A WAN may consist of a combination of microwaves, dedicated lease lines and satellite communications. Individual business firm may maintain their own WAN.

SPOTLIGHT

Insurance companies in India offer various services to the customer with the help of a network. Customer has to pay monthly, quarterly or yearly premium to the insurance companies. The company offers different types of policies to the customer. Premium is paid for a fixed number of years and after maturity, a customer receives the amount invested together with the bonus thereof. The insurance company informs and reminds the customer about the due date of premium, the bonus accumulated to their account, etc. The basic problem faced by a customer was when he changed his or her place of residence. The policy is opened by the insurance agent in the branch nearest to the customer. The premium is deposited in the branch as per policy. Another problem was that the customer had to wait at the counter to deposit the premium and it was also not possible to pay premium in another branch of the insurance company.

The problem of deposit has been solved with the help of the Local Area Network. Insurance companies have developed the client-server Local Area Network in the branches, where many computers are connected with the server. So a customer can deposit premium at any counter, as any computer can access data from the server, where all data are stored.

To solve the second case, an insurance company today connects most of its branches throughout the city with the help of a Wide Area Network. The Wide Area Network allows a customer to pay premium at any branch in any location provided the branch is connected under the Wide Area Network. In addition, all the information relating to that policy can be made available to the customer irrespective of the location of the branch.

The customer can therefore deposit premium at any counter of any branch. The computerized branch allows the customer to deposit the premium and also offer information relating to that policy.

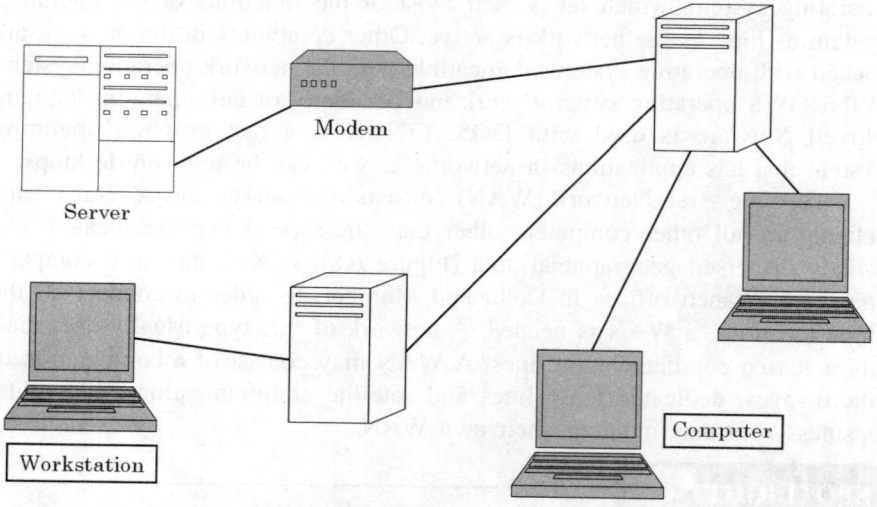

Figure 6.8 Wide Area Network.

Network management is a difficult task that needs attention in responding to the needs of users. There are many factors, which are important to a network management. The networks, which are accessed by the customers, like the Automated Teller Machine (ATM), are different from the one which a retail store manager uses. Performance is one of the important criteria used to measure users' satisfaction. Response time is the users' primary measure of network performance. The second objective of network management is to find cost-effective solutions to the problems.

Network management is also concerned with modular expansion cost, relocation of equipment, replacement cost, etc. Network availability is critically important to user satisfaction. Reliability refers to the probability that the network will continue to operate over a given period. Network management is a subject of academic study. Today number of courses are available on network management. With the advancement in technology of the computer systems, the network technology is also galloping at the same pace.

REVIEW QUESTIONS

1. What are the differences between conducted and radiated media?
2. List three ways that personal computers can be used as terminals.
3. Which conducted medium is the least expensive?
4. Name and briefly describe each of the conducted communication media in a communication system.
5. What is network topology? Discuss the star, ring and bus topologies.
6. What do you understand by Wide Area Network?
7. What is a geosynchronous orbit?
8. Briefly discuss the concept of Local Area Network and its applications.
9. What causes errors in microwave transmissions?
10. What do you understand by business data communication?

DISCUSSION QUESTIONS

1. What are the principal factors to consider when developing a telecommunication plan?
2. A firm has decided to build a Local Area Network in the office headquarters. You have been assigned to work with an engineer on plans for making the system capable of supporting the computing and telecommunication needs. What factors should you consider in design of the system?

7
Application of Information Systems

7.1 APPLICATION IN MANUFACTURING SECTOR

This chapter will introduce the role of Management Information Systems (MIS) in business (Figure 7.1). Each organization has its own Standard Operating Procedure (SOP). In a manufacturing set-up, the organization has two distinct, different functions. The first one is manufacturing, which deals with the goods being manufactured at shop-floor, raw materials, machines, workers and the factory set-up as a whole. The factory has store, maintenance, and production systems. In addition, the factory also deals with factory accounting and payroll.

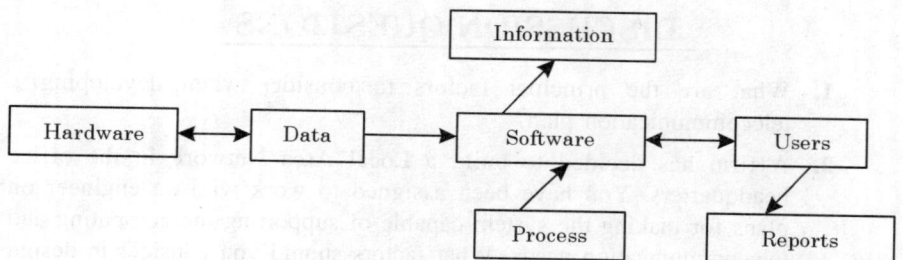

Figure 7.1 MIS components.

The second function is that of the head office and the regional offices which deal with paper information, rather than the product. In general, the head office consists of sales/marketing division, purchase division, accounts/finance and corporate human resources divisions. The organization may run two different systems to manage information. In a small or medium size company, it is not always feasible to invest in information technology resources. As a result, the other functional areas use the same data.

The reports are produced by MIS for the following purposes:

(a) Statutory reports
(b) Operation updates
(c) Action reports
(d) Knowledge updates
(e) Decision support

7.2 MARKETING INFORMATION SYSTEM

Marketing management functions deal with customers (Figure 7.2). In marketing, the input comes through the following subsystems:

(a) Accounting data entry—sales, payments, invoices, delivery notes.
(b) Market research data—industrial production, industrial survey.
(c) Market intelligence data—competitors' information.

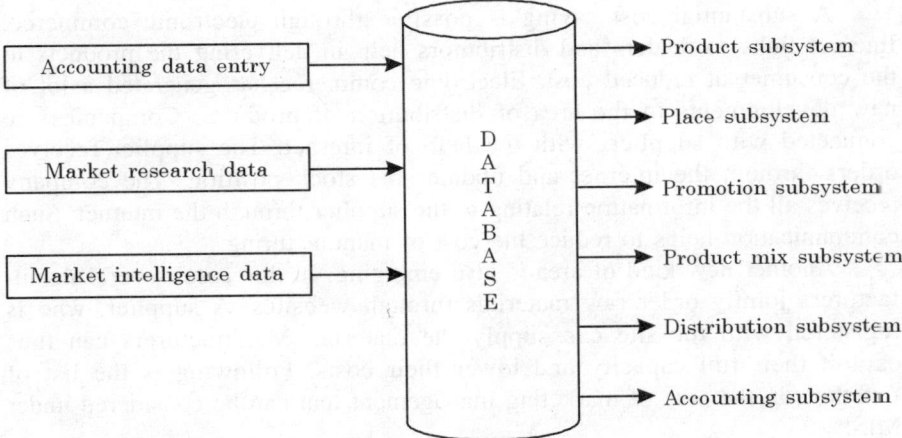

Figure 7.2 Marketing information system.

The reports are generated from those input data. The company may have a relational database system. Data may be stored in different places for the generation of the reports. The output subsystem consists of the followings:

(a) Product subsystem—sales value, customer, inventory.
(b) Place subsystem—zone, area, market segment.
(c) Promotion subsystem—dealer, commission
(d) Product mix subsystem—product, family.
(e) Distribution subsystem—distributor, dealer.
(f) Accounting subsystem—receivables, excise duty, tax.

The inputs on the left side of Figure 7.2 generate reports under the subsystems on the right side of the figure. For example, the inputs for the product subsystem come from accounting data entry. The reports are used for decision-making. The reports that can be generated are as follows:

Operational level

(a) Product sales ledger
(b) Accounting receivables
(c) Ageing reports
(d) Market and competition analysis
(e) Complaints of the customers
(f) Inventory reports

Decision/Control level

(a) Sales vs. sales forecast
(b) Expenses vs. projected expenses
(c) Market share
(d) Competitors' information

A substantial cost saving is possible through electronic commerce. Internet links to dealers and distributors help in delivering the products to the consumer at reduced cost. Electronic commerce has generated a lot of new developments in the area of distribution of products. Companies are connected with suppliers with the help of internet. The supplier receives orders through the internet and updates his stock position. The company receives all the information relating to the supplier through the internet. Such communication helps to reduce the cost of manufacturing.

Another new kind of area is also emerging. In this case, several manufacturers jointly order raw materials through websites. A supplier, who is registered with the site can supply the material. Manufacturers can thus exploit their full capacity and lower their costs. Following is the list of functions in the area of marketing management that can be considered under MIS:

(a) Demand planning: Understanding the customer requirement
(b) Order execution: Accurate demand plans
(c) Capacity planning: Optimal capacity usage
(d) Materials planning: Supply alignment
(e) Purchasing: Lowest total cost

7.3 FINANCIAL INFORMATION SYSTEM

The primary objective of a financial information system is to meet the financial needs of the business. It requires working capital management, long-term fund management with the goal of minimum cost of capital. The second objective is to meet statutory compliance, like the audited result declaration, obligation to government, tax authorities, banks and shareholders. Financial management includes the accounting system of the day-to-day functions. The financial budget is prepared in the beginning of the financial year. The financial department receives inputs from the following areas (Figure 7.3):

(a) Accounting information—invoice, voucher, journal entry.
(b) Audit, tax subsystem—sales tax, excise, income tax.
(c) Financial analysis data—EVA, ROI, stock market data, EPS.

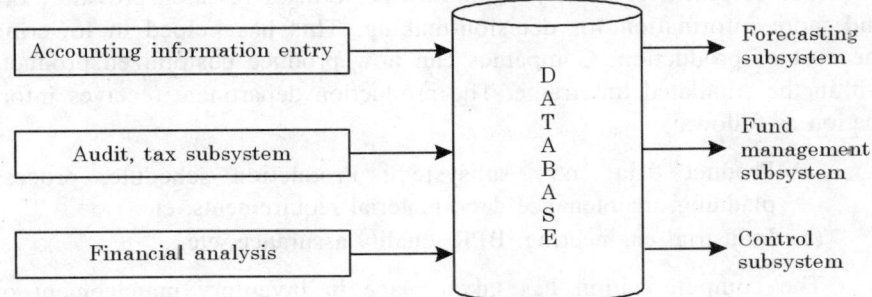

Figure 7.3 Financial information system.

Several inputs come from stores, marketing, and personnel department. These inputs generate the following outputs:

(a) Forecasting subsystem: Sales forecast, expenses, capital expenditure, etc.
(b) Fund management subsystem: Source and uses of funds, cash flow analysis, long-term fund management.
(c) Control subsystem: Budget, performance ratio, etc.

These output subsystems can generate the following reports for the management information system (MIS).

Operational level

(a) Statutory returns and reports
(b) Ledger, trial balance, balance sheet, etc.
(c) Registers—sales tax, excise
(d) Stock reports
(e) Accounts receivable and payable
(f) Bank and cash statements
(g) Aging reports

Decision/Control level

(a) Return on investments
(b) Cash flow analysis
(c) Break-even analysis

(d) Economic value addition analysis
(e) Ratio analysis
(g) Stock market information

7.4 PRODUCTION INFORMATION SYSTEM

The objective of the production management is to manufacture products on time with a stipulated quality. Production management has spent a long time in the development of society. Inputs in the form of research provide more and more information for decision-making. This has helped in lowering the cost of production. Companies can now produce customized products within the stipulated timeframe. The production department receives information as follows:

(a) Product data entry subsystem: Production schedule, process planning, maintenance data, material requirements, etc.
(b) Industrial engineering: BPR, quality assurance, etc.

The computerization has taken place in inventory management of manufactured stores. Material resources planning system was the computerisation of the production system. The following subsystems generate the required outputs (Figure 7.4):

(a) Production subsystem: Load status, job schedule, production schedule, etc.
(b) Inventory subsystem: Availability of materials, purchase requisitions.
(c) Quality subsystem: Quality control, inspection reports.
(d) Cost subsystem: Cost of raw materials, capital cost of machinery, labour cost, etc.

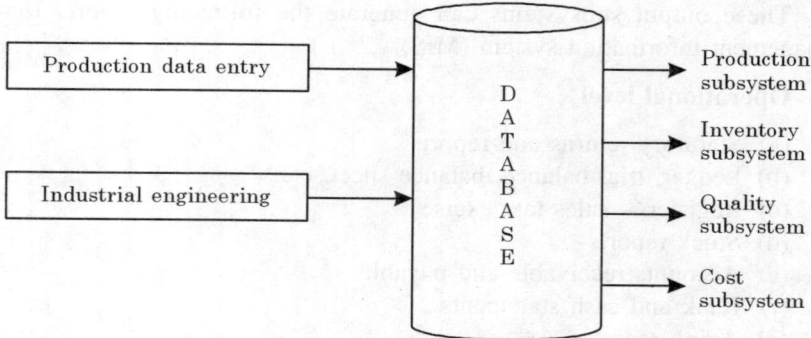

Figure 7.4 Production information system.

These subsystems can generate reports for the users of the systems. The reports could be as follows:

Operational level

(a) Materials requirement reports
(b) Breakdown reports
(c) Maintenance reports
(d) Consumption of power, fuel and consumables
(e) Utilization of machines and facilities
(f) Quality control reports

Decision/Control level

(a) Manufacture or subcontract
(b) Alternative process
(c) Product mix or job mix
(d) Technology update reports
(e) Consumption of power, fuel, and labour compared to industry
(f) Research and development
(g) The reports of the suppliers and vendors

Material management is another separate division in manufacturing. The product consists of around 30–45 of the raw material cost, depending on the nature of the product. Control of raw material is a distinct function of the material manager. Quality management starts from the raw material inspection process. Vendor development is another aspect of material management function.

7.5 HUMAN RESOURCE INFORMATION SYSTEM

The primary function of a human resource management is to provide manpower with specific abilities, skills and knowledge from time to time. In addition to training, benefits and compensation management, human resource management can be segregated into two functions. The first function is the attendance system and manpower administration. In the attendance system, human resource management is concerned with daily attendance and leave management. Attendance computerization is done in the first phase in leave management. Payroll management system is linked with attendance. The second function deals with benefits, an essential requirement at the management systems. One area that is not still computerized in many organizations is the workforce management. But the internet has opened new doors to human resource professionals. Recruitment cost has come down. It is possible to register for a job through the company's website. In many organizations, e-HR is successful. Even employees can input their own tour and travelling details from anywhere in the world. As a result, human resource people can make themselves free from accounting entry and can concentrate more on strategic level. They can simply put notices on website, where anyone can access at any time. Following are the input data entry systems (Figure 7.5):

(a) Accounting information: Attendance, payroll administration, etc.
(b) HR research system: Manpower planning, training, environmental reporting, etc.
(c) Virtual HR data entry: e-HR, e-recruitment, virtual employee management

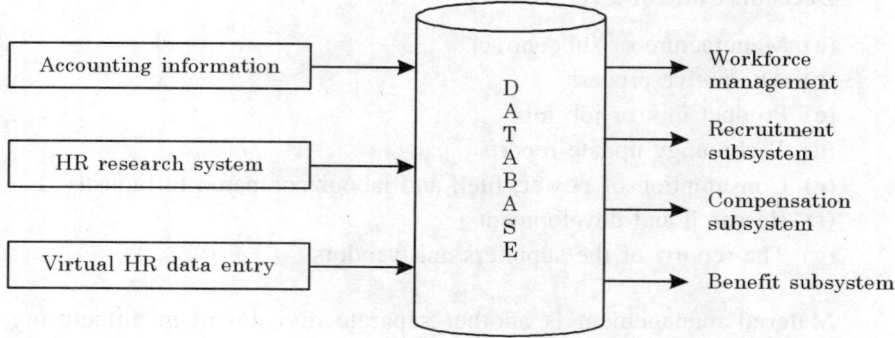

Figure 7.5 Human resource information systems.

These input data can generate reports under different subsystems. Those subsystems are listed below:

(a) Workforce management: Attendance monitoring, leave, manpower, job allocation (permanent and casual) report
(b) Recruitment subsystem: Internal search, hiring and application status management
(c) Compensation subsystem: Compensation management, liaison with government and other agencies
(d) Benefit subsystem: Provident fund, medical benefits, super-annuation, loans and deduction

All the subsystems may not be fully computerized. Subsystems receive inputs and produce reports for decision-making.

Operational level

(a) Daily attendance system
(b) Strength under different category, like, trainee, casual, permanent, etc.
(c) Cost of employee to the company
(d) Workload distribution
(e) Leave management report
(f) Training report

Decision/Control level

(a) Manpower projection and planning
(b) Training need and development
(c) Job analysis
(d) Recruitment process
(e) Compensation analysis

e-HR is gaining popularity in India. Most companies receive applications through e-mail. It not only saves substantial time but also the cost of recruit-ment. HR manuals, policy matters, notifications can be posted on websites. It saves a lot of paper work and cost. Many companies offer online interview through the internet.

7.6 BUSINESS PROCESS OUTSOURCING (BPO)

The dictionary meaning of the word 'outsource' is to arrange goods and services from outside of the company. Outsourcing is transcending its traditional IT and data processing boundaries. The growth rate of business process outsourcing is outstripping that of the IT arena. We see significant growth in such areas as logistics, human resources, building facilities management and back office accounting services.

Outsourcing takes place when an organization transfers the ownership of a business process to a supplier. The key to this definition is the aspect of transfer of control. This definition differentiates outsourcing from business relationships in which the buyer retains the control of the process or, in other words, tells the supplier how to do the work. It is the transfer of ownership that defines outsourcing and often makes it such a challenging and painful process. In outsourcing, the buyer (outsourcer) does not instruct the supplier how to perform its task, instead, focuses on communicating what results the buyer wants to buy; it leaves the process of accomplishing those results to the sole discretion of the supplier(s).

Today, outsourcing has become a strategy for forward-thinking managers. It is no longer just a means for reducing costs, but a tool for adding value to business. It enables organizations to concentrate on their core business operations, carry out business re-engineering and provide information that is valid, timely and adequate to assist in decision-making at the top management level and quality and cost control at the middle and lower levels.

The outsourcing was restricted within and outside the country in terms of product in the manufacturing sector. In manufacturing sector, when raw materials or inputs of the product are outsourced, it requires proximity to the factory, otherwise the cost may increase. Sourcing brings many economic benefits. Cheaper materials and labour bring down the production cost. This makes companies competitive and profitable, and lower prices increase the demand of the products. Companies spend their profits on improving the existing products and introducing the new ones. Customers buy more of the things they already consume, or spend the money on new goods and services. This stimulates innovation and creates new jobs in the market.

Business processes of an organization are the unique tasks which aim at attaining the overall organizational objectives. These business processes can be classified into four broad categories, known as (Figure 7.6):

(1) Product process
(2) Service process
(3) Customer centric process
(4) Quality control process

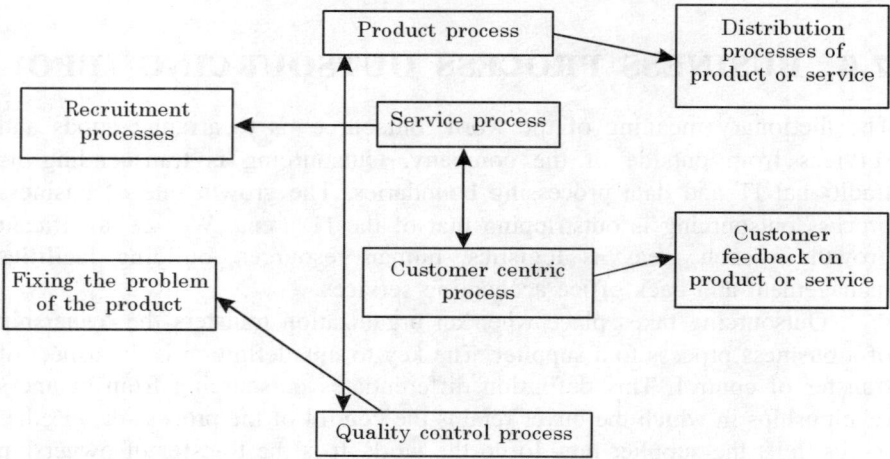

Figure 7.6 Business process outsourcing.

Almost all these segments of business can qualify to be outsourced. But not all of them are equally conspicuous in terms of prevailing business opportunities. For instance, currently, the call centres are in vogue. But apart from that, some other segments like R&D and manufacturing sector outsourcing are also coming up with huge business potential. Some of the processes, which are in vogue in the outsourcing sector are listed below:

(1) Finance and accounting (settlement accounts, credit/debit card)
(2) Marketing and its subprocesses (i.e. call centre, tele-sales)
(3) Health care (i.e. medical transcriptions, etc.)
(4) Human resources (i.e. skilled labour)
(5) Information technology (i.e. call centre, solution provider, etc.)
(6) Manufacturing (i.e. engineering, etc.)
(7) R&D (i.e. testing, bio-genetic research, etc.)

The prices of the finished products are so competitive that the companies are forced to outsource. It is cost-effective to outsource a product or service rather than produce it in-house. Here, we take a glance at the cost units of the BPO concerns. The major elements of the BPO costs are:

- Manpower
- General and administration
- Telecommunication
- Property rentals
- Depreciation of equipment

The manpower and property costs are much lower in developing or underdeveloped countries compared to those in developed countries. In addition, technical and skilled manpower is also available in developing countries at lower costs. India has a significant advantage in terms of skilled labour and tele-communication infrastructure.

Any business process outsourcing job received from the outside is termed *offshore business*. Offshore centre refers to a centre that is located in a foreign country and is primarily used for inbound service. Not all kinds of projects can be outsourced from offshore locations. It depends entirely upon the nature and scope of the respective functionalities and processes involved in them. Following are the projects that can be out-sourced offshore with tremendous benefits:

(1) Telephone answering service
(2) Account status
(3) Payroll services
(4) Inbound call centre services
(5) Outbound telemarketing services
(6) Claims reporting
(7) Emergency notification
(8) Credit collections/debt collections
(9) Mortgage marketing
(10) Voice messaging service
(11) Invoice payment
(12) 1600 toll-free services and call back systems
(13) Product ordering and fulfilment
(14) Interactive voice response service
(15) Inventory services
(16) Calling card services
(17) Inbound telemarketing services
(18) Appointment reminders
(19) Insurance marketing
(20) Real estate marketing

A BPO arrangement can fetch significant economic benefits for the outsourcing nations. These benefits can be depicted as follows:

- Productivity improvement
- Access to expertise
- Operational cost control
- Cost savings
- Opportunity to focus on the core business area

As discussed earlier, outsourcing helps companies save cost directly and it also gives return in terms of other factors of an oraganization as listed below.

Benefits of Outsourcing

- Increased sales and profits
- Reduced costs per sale
- Maximum phone productivity
- Increased number of appointments
- Increased customer base
- Increased lead generation
- Higher number of qualified leads
- Higher number of closed sales
- Better customer retention
- More immediate feedback
- Better results through test marketing
- Increased local, regional, or national market share

Technology

Technology is one of the major areas needed for the companies which manage business process outsourcing. Using the state-of-the-art technology and fully automated equipment, centres have a considerable competitive advantage to offer to the organizations. The latest technological solutions are designed to provide the knowledge needed to develop effective customer strategies and maximize customer profitability.

- CRM solutions
- IVR systems
- CTI software
- ACD
- Windows over web
- Call recording solutions and call monitoring solutions
- Predictive dialling
- Soft phone
- Text-to-speech software
- Voice recognition
- Programmable/soft switches

Customer Relationship Management (CRM) solutions facilitate firms to create the customer relationship needed to uncover new business opportunities and enhance client service. The solutions are designed to provide the knowledge needed to develop effective customer strategies and maximize customer profitability. CRM solutions deliver the robust functionality needed to achieve maximum return on customer relationships. Giving accurate and timely information is of extreme significance to call centre operations. CRM solutions are ideally suited for call centres. These solutions have increased the productivity of call centres, also providing a reliable presentation of their critical product and customer information.

The CRM software has the power and flexibility to manage virtually any call centre operation, no matter how large or small. Starting with database and development tools, the software contains a CRM application including telephony and web integration and a complete call centre phone system.

Interactive Voice Response (IVR) system is designed to make it easy to configure automated call handling systems that can be tailored to individual needs. This comprehensive system leads to distribution of routing information with the help of FAX or pre-recorded voice messages. It includes services like:

- Speech recognition
- Self-service
- Fax management capabilities

It is also very handy in reducing fatigue, increasing efficiency and decreasing the time spent by agents in imparting information. Organizations who are looking for reducing costs and improving customer service can contract their inbound phone and outbound voice messaging programs at the IVR call centres. The IVR outsourcing services provide a competitive advantage in the marketplace and make the inbound telemarketing services, affordable. Voice broadcasting clients can download voice recordings and call lists and even manage the start and end of their calling campaigns that operate at the IVR call centre. Users can view call campaign reports and the percentage of completion. To achieve the maximum results from IVR and voice broadcasting phone programs, it is advisable to use professional voice recording services. The voice recordings can be produced in minimal time at a professional recording.

CTI software or Computer Telephony Integration (CTI) software is the advanced technology that serves as the focal point of the working of modern centres. It integrates the organization's computer and telephone systems and facilitates effective applications to make every phone call, inbound and outbound. Although the most widely-known CTI application is screen population or screen pop, CTI is also used by applications including:

- Quality monitoring
- E-mail management

- Predictive dialling
- CRM

The CTI software is a rich set of phone software library routines that enable the application programs to control the phone system. It helps increase employee productivity, enhance customer service and reduce costs by combining the capabilities of the phone system with the custom functionality of Windows, Unix or Web applications. Data collected by the phone ACD (Automatic Call Distribution) or IVR (Interactive Voice Response) systems can be passed to the PC, Unix or Web applications through the phone software.

Automated Call Distribution (ACD) facilitates control the distribution of telephone calls coming into the department. ACD systems are call routing utilities for incoming calls and can be even used to route calls originated by the predictive dialler to the next available agent. The staff log the in/out of the ACD system as they became available, and the system answers the calls and distributes them. When staff is not available, the ACD system holds a call in queue and then forwards it to the first available staff member.

Automatic call distribution is ideal for areas where multiple staff answers a high volume of calls, e.g. Help desk, Appointment scheduling, Message taking, etc.

Managing calls properly can be the key in providing excellent customer service, and the ACD system provides the tools needed to optimally manage incoming calls. Some of the tools an ACD system offers like customizing the way its staff answers calls using several variables, including the caller's location (on-campus or off-campus, local or long distance) or the purpose of the call (help assistance, appointment scheduling).

Windows Over Web (WOW) or the thin-client technology brings to the front, a new approach to program and undertake application development. The technology is known as 'thin-client technology' as it reduces the software resources and computer hardware needed at each individual desktop. Thin clients use centralized software provided over internal networks to serve a combination of PCs, Windows-based terminals and other network computing resources. Cost savings also result from less frequent desktop servicing requirements caused by software and hardware conflicts or installation problems. WOW technology greatly helps remote agents and home-based support centres. With secure applications, employees can work from remote offices and from the convenience of their homes using the same applications that are running in the office. Thin-client technology helps enterprises in the following ways:

- Reduction in costs
- Increased security
- Quick deployment
- Improved manageability

It offers a viable alternative to the desktop PC for many, making access to business data and applications easy, secure and affordable. With a thin-client system, the client sends keystrokes and mouse movements to the server over the network or dial-up connection, and the server sends back changes in the display. Any PC can be a client, but because very little processing is performed at the desktop, businesses can also use low-cost terminals that have no moving parts (no hard drive) and a generally small amount of memory (RAM). Since each client is just a terminal, all data and settings, even the applications are on the server. To back up everything for all the users, the organization only needs to back up the server. And for disaster recovery, backups are easier and more centralized, making it easier to take the backups off-site.

Call recording and monitoring solutions help to train the agents and improve customer service. They are designed to be a complete call centre solution including predictive dialling, ACD, IVR, and digital voice recording. Call recording plays a significant role and helps in monitoring agent performance while performing quality assurance tasks. Order entry verification and confirmation can be easily accomplished when the calls are recorded. Call centres can thus, record and retrieve phone conversations in real time. The recording can be customized to meet virtually any set of business rules.

Predictive dialler is a computer-based dialogic predictive dialling system that handles inbound and outbound phone calls. It brings about cost savings, improved control, maximized productivity and efficient use of resources. The system automatically dials the telephone for telemarketers and connects only the live voice contacts. It does this by listening and filtering out the answering machines, busy signals, operator interceptions and other types of non-functional calls. Telemarketers no longer waste time dialling numbers or listening to no answers—all they do is talk to prospects. A complex mathematical formula (predictive algorithm) is used that predicts when each telemarketer becomes available, allowing the telemarketers to flow seamlessly from one call to the next. Calls are either initiated by the phone system or accepted from the outside and distributed in an intelligent fashion to service agents using ACD systems. The process thus, improves the telemarketing production as it doubles the amount of contacts that telemarketers make per day.

Soft phone is an ideal solution for employees who are out of the office, frequently travelling on business, workers that work both at home and office as well as those who require the interaction of data with their work such as a remote ACD agent.

Soft phone includes features like:

- Caller-ID
- Call waiting
- Transfer
- Hold

- Conferencing
- Voice mail capability

The soft phone functions on the LAN over the Internet, enabling the employees to work either in corporate offices, satellite remote offices or from the convenience of home. The soft phone system can be used to generate real time reports and the important graphics measuring system helps serve and control the performance of the phone system with clear and meaningful displays. Graphs and charts of operational statistics help to measure the effectiveness of each user campaign. Reports and graphs include both inbound and outbound statistics.

Text-to-speech software is used to convert words from a computer document (e.g. word processor document, web page) into audible speech spoken through the computer speaker. The text-to-speech software reads the text words with different voices that can be chosen. The text words may be on the screen, in the clipboard, from a text file or some other source. The technology synthesizes the natural sounding speech from ordinary text. The text can just be copied to the clipboard or imported from text files. The software then reads the text to the user or converts the text to MP3 or WAV file. It also allows the conversion of text into a MP3/WAV audio file that can be listened later.

The text-to-speech software has the capability to extract variable information from a database (or from the Web) that is later converted into audible speech. The applications of the software include:

- Providing callers with account information
- Weather updates
- Sports scores
- Stored text messages

Voice recognition software allows the system to recognize keywords or phrases from a caller. Voice recognition is an excellent application to aid callers who do not have access to the touchtone keypad or are using rotary phones. Enhanced voice recognition functionality promises lower costs, facilitates the agents to handle only those calls that require human intervention. There are multiple types of voice recognition facilities such as:

- Discrete numeric
- Continuous numeric
- Alphanumeric
- Speaker dependent
- Custom

It makes a voiceprint of customers' voices and enables the call centre to automatically recognize customers each time they call. This is done once the call centre has programmed the voices into the system. Instead of pressing prompts on a telephone keypad, the customer can speak requests and the system can automate them, reducing the burden on call centre representatives. An administrator sets the tolerance thresholds that will alert a call centre agent if a person falls below the threshold of probability, adding another layer of security to customer accounts. Voice recognition systems help machines to understand a caller's voice and extract meanings from the words. Callers do not have to say specific words such as 'collect' or 'refund' for the technology to understand the meaning of the caller's request. The machine gets a transcription of the text of the customer's request and attempts to classify the request. Depending on the caller's need, help could be provided by a human agent or an interactive voice response system.

Programmable switches are becoming increasingly important weapons used by Internet telephony providers to bridge the gap between IP and circuit-switched protocols. Programmable switches operate seamlessly within traditional network infrastructure and provide a path for transmission between two communication devices and the routing of information between them.

Programmable switches serve as flexible solutions for network operators. They are the multi-protocol application for intelligent networks and are applicable as gateway and for conversion of protocols. With these switches, customization can be done on an application-by-application basis, thereby giving service providers the ability to differentiate their service from the competition, quickly and cost effectively.

Through openness and configurability, programmable switches have the versatility to provide a platform for multi-service applications. They offer a superior return on investment owing to their excellent price performance and also enable more capacity. Thus, a service provider can support a larger subscriber population and consequently, receive greater revenue per configuration. These programmable switches are flexible and adaptable and thus deliver a greater versatility of function per system.

Thus a firm which engages in outsourcing is in a better position to concentrate on its core competencies. But alternatively, a firm can do business without indulging into outsourcing if the firm has enough affordability and scope to vertically integrate the business on a larger scale. But, still it is better for a firm to go for outsourcing at the present socio-economic situation of the world. As we have mentioned earlier, firms engaged in outsourcing can reap fortunes, especially through the following ways:

- It reduces the overhead cost in having to maintain a full-time employee.
- It enables you to concentrate your resources on marketing.
- It facilitates the optimum usage of time.
- The production cost will be cheaper if outsourced to developing nations, making the product price competitive.
- It provides opportunity to deal with an established company that you can depend on more than a freelancer.

REVIEW QUESTIONS

1. What are the functions of marketing information systems?
2. What are the functions of financial information systems?
3. What are the functions of production information systems?
4. What are the functions of human resources information systems?
5. Discuss in detail business process outsourcing (BPO) in the light of Indian context.

DISCUSSION QUESTIONS

1. Information has become a key input in the manufacturing industry. Discuss this statement with suitable examples from the manufacturing industry.
2. Application software development requires domain expertise. What are your views in the light of Indian service industry?

8

Organization and Information System

8.1 RELATIONSHIP BETWEEN ORGANIZATION AND INFORMATION SYSTEM

Information system has been changing the organization not only by effecting reduction in the number of levels but also by changing the way of working. By definition, **organization** is a social entity with direct goal and activities which are structured in a way that are linked with external environment. Organizations produce goods and services that customers want at competitive prices. Companies look for innovative ways to produce and distribute goods and services most efficiently. Redesigning organizational structures and management practices can also contribute to increase in efficiency. Organizations help in creating innovations rather than keep relying on standard products and automated ways of doing things. Standard Operating Procedure (SOP) is laid down by committee or government in the case of public sector. It has a long-term effect on the organization. Companies in the same business may have different standard procedures for working. Now the area of concern is the effect on suppliers in the event of change in procedure. This is part of the organization culture, that is, a set of fundamental assumptions about the organization. The set of fundamental assumptions are about service to customers, myths, behaviour of employees, etc. That is, how to produce, where to produce, for whom to produce, etc. Employees are indoctrinated with all those procedures to work with. A newly recruited employee is trained and then inducted into the department or division for working.

The flow of information system depends on the culture that is prevalent at the organization. Two organizations cannot have similar cultures. Automation has changed the culture of the organization but not the information.

So, the standard operating process may change with the same information flow. But it is not true for all cases.

Computerization in the organizations has been changing and affecting them directly. When we see the caption "Fully Computerized Bank Branch", the message has a clear-cut difference. Do the customers perceive these organizations differently? It is a learning process through which both the organization and the customers are educating themselves. Here the organization has to change or adopt the changes to adjust to this situation. During this process of learning, the organization reflects the desire to improve in all relevant areas. Computer-aided manufacturing and new information technology also help promote innovation. The information system is also a part of the external environmental influence on the organization. In the banking industry, the changes taken place are so enormous that many of them are of international standard. The direct impact of information technology is evident in many branches. Most activities are managed today through information technology. Through all these activities, organizations create value for their owners, customers and employees.

SPOTLIGHT

At a bank, a customer used to wait for two hours for a draft. His savings account was updated manually by the bank officer. The bank recently announced "Fully Computerized Branch", with much fanfare. The bank-teller counter services the customer in the same way. The passbook is now updated by a computer printer. The draft is prepared in the same way, except that it is printed by a computer. Bank employees have not changed their attitudes, though each one has a computer on his or her desk. The front office information flow has not changed. The back office information management has changed. The end result, the bank has increased its banking hours.

Figure 8.1 shows many mediating factors that influence the interaction between the organization and information technology.

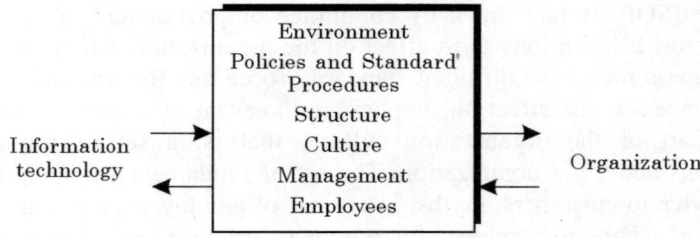

Figure 8.1 Organization and information system.

The organization is part of the information processing system, though most organizations are not primarily designed for information processing. Behavioural factors have many implications over other factors. So, the changed management process and the change agent play an important role to develop the information system. According to the behavioural view of the firm, people in the organizations develop customary ways of working; they develop attachment to colleagues and a work culture. The introduction of new technology changes the way input is converted to output. Thus, building new information systems or rebuilding old involves many changes in technical rearrangement of machines or workers. The technical changes require a change that controls and owns information. The firm is seen as infinitely malleable with labour and capital, substituting for one another easily. The behavioural and technical definition of organizations is complementary to each other. The organizational culture changes with the technology. Employees are trained and inducted into the organization. It is necessary to change the operating procedures as the technology changes. In the long run, the culture takes a new dimension to provide services to the customers. The technological theories tell us how firms in a competitive environment combine capital and labour and information technology, whereas the behaviour model tells us how individuals play their role with the adaptation of information technology. Some information technology systems change the rights, privileges, obligations, responsibilities and feelings that have been established over a long period of time.

8.2 EFFECTS OF ORGANIZATION ON INFORMATION SYSTEM

Organizations have an impact on information system by the decision-making process of the employees. Technology refers to the tools, techniques, machines and actions used to transform input into output. Technology is an organization's production process and includes procedures and machinery. Managers decide who will build and operate the system and also provide the rationale for building systems. Let us discuss now how application of information system has been taking place in the firm from inception of this technology. The last five decades have noticed dramatic changes in technology and organization. During the 1950s, few functions like accounts receivable/payable, payroll, general ledger were computerized. Organizations were dependent on a few critical functions. In the 1960s, systems like budget, marketing, manufacturing were developed. By the late 1970s and 1980s, information became complex and the telecommunications technology was added. The functions like simulation, decision support system, office automation, forecasting became possible to be programmed through the information system. During the 1990s, information architecture was developed as an enterprisewide information utility. New areas like central data management, enterprise resource management, distributed processing, etc. were evolved. From 1995 onwards information management took another new dimension with the birth of Internet. E-commerce has been implemented by many organizations. The end result is an enormous change in organizational structure and culture. The information system had become integral, online, and an interactive tool deeply involved in minute-to-minute operations and decision-making of large organizations. Today, organizations are critically dependent on systems and cannot survive occasional breakdowns. The development process is continuous and fast compared to other technological developments. As a result, the organizations have been adopting the latest technology.

A second way in which the organizations affect information technology is the decision-making process. New kinds of positions were created like programmers, system analysts, database administrators, and information system managers. The computer system is basically composed of three distinct entities. The first is a formal unit called the information system department. The second consists of the information specialist. A third element is the technology itself, both hardware and software. Today information system unit acts as a change agent, suggesting new business areas and information-based products with planned changes in the organizations.

The relation between a new technology and organization seems to follow a pattern, beginning with immediate effects on the content of jobs followed by impact on the design of the organization. Job description has changed and individuals are empowered more with the implementation of information technology. The hierarchy has taken different shapes depending on industry and secondly on products. Various studies show a flat pattern in the middle layer of the hierarchy compared to the flat structure in the lower level. New kind of business like call centre, medical transcription have totally different hierarchies. Knowledge workers have changed the structure of the organization. Technology, by empowering the individual has changed the organizational politics. An individual, even at a junior level, can take decisions and is empowered to implement. In organizational politics, the distribution of power has been taking a new dimension.

The ultimate impact of technology on employees can be understood through a hierarchical structure. In addition to actually replacing human workers, information technology may have several different effects on jobs that remain. It has helped on job simplification, which means the variety and difficulty of tasks performed by a single person has reduced. On the other hand, the job provides greater responsibility, recognition and opportunities for growth and development. So, it tends to cause job enrichment.

Today information technology is essential in Supply Chain Management (SCM), Customer Relationship Management (CRM) and electronic online trading. The interesting factor is that the customer is also empowered to take decisions.

The organizational hierarchy is formed keeping in view the objectives. In many cases, a whole group manages different functions like distribution, payment, content development and partner management. But the individual is responsible to the authority to implement the function assigned to him as a team member.

> **SPOTLIGHT**
>
> A company manufactures an air pollution control system for industry like coal, cement, power, etc. The company sells two products—the dust suppression system and the dust extraction system. The company sells these products as part of a project. The company has 120 employees including workers. At the top level, the director is the owner and the CEO is the employee of the organization. The company performs functions such as project estimation, design, production and marketing. The marketing department first collects the projects and then hands them over to the project department. Each department has a senior level manager heading the department. In a recent development the CEO resigned. The CEO position was replaced by the General Manager. The new person resisted computerization in the organization. The end result was the re-orientation throughout the organization within one year after his joining. Many people resigned and were replaced by new employees. Changes also took place place in the hierarchy and job design. The support from the top management was obvious.

The information technology needs training and education of employee, because they need higher level skills and greater competence to master their tasks. As a result, it creates more opportunities for intellectual mastery and enhanced cognitive skill for workers. In other ways, it develops job enlargement. Employees are vested with more responsibilities for better results through greater interdependence among employees, development of teamwork and coordination skills.

8.3 IMPACT OF INFORMATION TECHNOLOGY ON ORGANIZATION DESIGN

Organization theory has been focusing continuously on the hierarchical responsibilities, job design, decision-making, etc. All types of organizations, small, medium scale and big, have changed with technological developments. Here we will put emphasis on the design of organizations. The developments in information technology are having a tremendous impact on all organizations in every industry. Information technology enables organizations to outsource various functions and use fewer in-house resources. It has a direct impact on small organizations. In the Internet-based business, there is no 'formal organization' in terms of building space and so forth. It enables organizations to work with fewer people, leading to a decline in the size of the organizations.

Has the information technology changed the design of the organization? The answers are many. Job design deals with individual responsibility, authority, position in the hierarchy, etc. The part of the job may be automated by information technology, while the remaining part may still be dependent on human touch. The risk associated with the failure of information technology is very high. In many cases, it is therefore recommended to work with the existing process. With this in view, organizational design is a much more complicated job than the human resources management. A failure of the ticket-counter computer which deals with a big queue will result in a huge loss to Railways. Control panel failures in a sophisticated conveyor belt of a pharmaceutical company may result in a huge financial loss to the company. Job design is the primary job, when information technology is in the forefront.

It is far more practical to analyse the job itself before redesigning the hierarchy of the organization. Otherwise it may fail to address the issue in the long run, which may cause failure of the organization.

SPOTLIGHT

Companies are cutting operating costs through outsourcing services. The costs of outsourcing from other vendors are lower. Call centres are working for different companies. Banking, investment, insurance, and even manufacturing companies avail services of call centres. The employees of those call centres offer information to the customers on behalf of the company. The customers are not aware of any other fact except the required information or services. Those people are empowered to take decisions and help customers. A company may lose customers because of the poor services offered by the call centres. Thus, the management of the organization may fail to understand the real cause of failure.

Advances in information technology have reduced the number of layers of management and decentralized the decision-making. Managers have the information spread in different geographical locations. They need to make important decisions quickly, rather than writing to headquarters. Today banks are offering service almost everywhere in India and it is possible to access from any location, where the branch is available. In this way, it has not only empowered the employees but also the whole job is redesigned. An organization may be made up of numerous small teams or even individuals who work autonomously but co-ordinate electronically. Information technology has improved the internal and external co-ordination. One of the greatest outcomes of information technology is perhaps its potential to improve co-ordination and communication both within the firm and with the other organizations. It enables the formation of networked organizations and other forms of organizational interdependence. With today's technology, employees can have instant access to the pertinent information about the job, allowing greater participation and autonomy. Technology will therefore continue to have a significant impact on organizational design.

REVIEW QUESTIONS

1. What is an organization?
2. Give three examples of external information sources.
3. Describe the three basic kinds of organization structures.
4. In what ways can an organization diverge?
5. Why do organizations adopt information systems?
6. Describe the different behavioural theories that explain how an information system affects the organization.
7. What is organization design?
8. What is the relationship between the information system and the organizational politics?
9. How do information systems change the organizational structure?

DISCUSSION QUESTIONS

1. When we design an information system, we redesign an organization. Discuss with examples.
2. In general, how do you view information—as textual, tabular or graphics?

9

System Analysis and Design

9.1 INTRODUCTION TO INFORMATION SYSTEM DEVELOPMENT

Organizations have their own methods and procedures. They are linked with purchase, customers, the suppliers and the inter-organizational system. Organizations have been changing their policies with the changes taking place in competition, environment, government policies, etc. It is not an easy task to keep pace with changes in time. Limited resources are the basic constraints to change. As a result, the development of a system is a continuous process in any organization. In business, System Analysis and Design (SAD) refers to the process of examining a business situation with a view to improving it through better procedures and methods.

The development of systems has two major components:

(1) System analysis
(2) System design

The concept is based on any existing or new system of development. It may happen that an organization likes to introduce a computerized compensation system. Earlier the process was manual comprising a four-day assignment. The job starts with the analysis of each process till it is distributed to the employees. Here at each point, the process is analysed to design the job. The job is designed in such way that the computerization is achieved. **System design** is the process of planning a new business system or replacing it or complementing the existing system. So, we must understand the old system thoroughly and determine how computers can be used to make it more effective. The process of gathering and interpreting facts, diagnosing problems and using the information to recommend improvements to the system is called **system analysis**. This is the job of a system analyst. The word "system" has been used several times throughout this chapter. In a broader sense, a **system** is a set of components that interact to accomplish some purpose. A business is also a system. Its components are manufacturing, marketing, finance, and personnel—towards the purpose of profit or value maximization of the organization. Each of those components itself is a system. A system consists of various subsystems.

SPOTLIGHT

An accounting system of any organization may consist of a cash flow system, a ledger management system, a debtors management system, etc. So, under a big system, one may find a number of subsystems. In an accounting system, data are entered by cash or bank entry, sale or purchase bill and journal entry. The output of the accounting system is used by finance to generate the cash flow statement. In another way, the data generates the debtors' statement. As a whole, debtors' management is a different task. So, other systems exist under the main system. Here, accounting is the system and cash flow, debtors, etc. are the subsystems.

Every business system depends more or less on an information system. This is the flow of data from one entity to another, and can encompass everything that can generate reports. An information system links all other systems and subsystems in such a way that they effectively work towards the same objective. It is interesting to note that in a manufacturing system, except production on the shop-floor, all other deliverables are pieces of information. We can talk about any other department except production and stores; mainly the other functional areas are those that deal with the information flow. The reports are developed and analysed for decision-making. Time is an important factor for decisions. So, the development of an information system is an area of importance and concern for any organization.

SPOTLIGHT

Let us look at a service industry; information flow plays a major part in banking, insurance and other service industries. In hotel industry, information is the key area for decision-making. In service industry, information designing is a very important part. Banks deal with money. But information technology disallows exchange of money in a traditional way for depositing in another branch. It is possible to transfer money to the other bank branch without physical transfer. In that case, information transfer plays the vital role, but not the physical money transfer.

Thus design and analysis of information is the key area for any kind of system development.

The system's purpose is its reason for existing. To achieve their purposes, systems interact with their environment, i.e., entities outside the boundary defined as **open systems**. In contrast, the systems that do not interact with their surroundings are called **closed systems**. All outgoing systems are open but the concept of the closed system exists as well.

The purposes of the information system are to process the input, produce information reports, maintain files, database and other outputs. An information system consists of hardware, software and data storage for files and database. The application of the information system deals with particular data, file and equipment. Here we are more focused on the organization rather than other environmental factors. An organization itself plays a major role in the development of the information system. The change throughout the globe in organizational works has been putting pressure on analysts to meet their objectives.

Several different types of information systems exist in an organization. There are transaction processing systems, management information systems, decision support systems, etc. A transaction is any event or an activity that affects organizations. Common transactions are billing, sales order, recruitment of people, etc. All firms process transactions as a major part of their activities. Information management is here to play an active role. The processed data on transactions are used as the input for Management Information Systems (MIS). The objective of the firm is to carry out transaction processing in an orderly and efficient manner. In the end, their management information system contributes to their decision support system. So, the job of the analyst is more critical to developing the processing system, which involves developing raw sources of data as well. This basis of development needs a lot of expertise and knowledge on this subject of information management. Thus, the analysis of the system plays a critical role in any system, which, in turn, helps the process of designing the system efficiently.

9.2 SYSTEM DEVELOPMENT METHODOLOGIES

In an organization, different types of systems are developed over a period of time. It may develop a new or experimental system or undertake reconstruction of an old system. There are many factors involved in developing a system. Here, we are more focused on the development of computerized information management systems. In some instances, the factor to be considered is an information system project, such as the computer aspect and communication technology and the impact of the new system on the employees in a firm, and the specific features of this system can therefore be determined in a proper fashion. In other instances, experience must be gained through experimentation at different stages. The interesting factor is that computers are being used by more and more persons who are not computer professionals, and the face of the development is taking an additional dimension. In addition, users themselves are installing software and adding more features to the systems they use.

Three different situations by three different approaches are used to represent the development of computer information systems. They are:

- System development life cycle method
- Structured analysis development method
- System prototype method.

System Development Life Cycle Method (SDLC)

The System Development Life Cycle Method (SDLC) is classically thought of as the set of activities that are carried out by the developer for the implementation of the information system. The development of an information system passes through different cycles or stages. Normally each phase starts after the preceding one is completed, but they are linked and necessary changes take place as required in the design and analysis phase. Moreover different parts of the project can be in various states at the same time, with some components undergoing analysis while the others being at design phase. The System Development Life Cycle Method (SDLC) consists of the following activities, as shown in Figure 9.1.

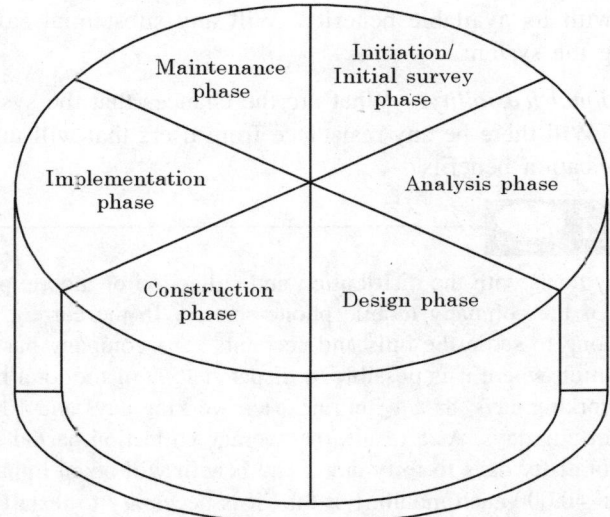

Figure 9.1 System Development Life Cycle Method (SDLC).

Initiation/initial survey phase

This phase starts when someone, either a user or a member of the system department suggests a data processing solution for a problem. Someone may come out with a new solution to an existing problem. In the initiation phase, the analyst does a preliminary study of the users' needs. The system developer studies the current system and puts forward a proposed solution with alternative solutions to be considered. In the same phase, an economic justification, basically the cost and benefit analysis is done. The schedule of time and cost estimates for the completion of the project is also taken care of at the preliminary stage. At this stage, the reports pass through senior levels based on the departments involved. Once this stage is through under various points of interaction, the system developer or analyst works towards the next stage. Here we use 'stage' and 'phase' interchangeably.

An important outcome of this stage is the determination that the system requested is feasible. Basically there are three aspects of the feasibility study.

- Technical feasibility
- Economic feasibility
- Operational feasibility

Technical feasibility: Will the project be possible with the existing software, hardware and the available software personnel? What is the likelihood that a new technology can be developed?

Economic feasibility: Are the costs involved acceptable in creating the system with its available benefits? Will any substantial savings accrue after creating the system?

Operational feasibility: What are the chances that the system will not get rejected? Will there be any resistance from users that will undermine the possible application benefits?

SPOTLIGHT

A company deals with the distribution and collection of mobile phone bills on behalf of the company mobile phone service. In the current system, it takes too long to settle the bills and accounts. The company has come out with a solution where it is possible to dispatch 15% of the total bills in the first five working days, 85% within next ten working days and 100% within next 15 working days. As a result, the average collection period should get reduced from fifty days to forty days. The benefit will be an improved cash flow of Rs. 40,000 each month. For this, it is necessary to install two more computers with a new network-based package. The same manpower can be distributed with one-time training. The system needs a further investment of Rs. 125,000. The feasibility study shows that the recurring benefits are much more than the initial fixed cost.

The technical and operational feasibility may show that the project is favourable and beneficial to the user. Normally the technological changes required may offer some resistance to system development. But the feasibility study helps to identify the blocks before the commencement of the analysis stage. The organization may prefer to stop the project at this stage or allow the analyst to carry out a more detailed feasibility study.

Analysis phase

During the analysis phase, the analyst and the users come in close interaction on what functions the proposed system has to perform. Normally, the prepared report contains the details of the output to be produced, input that must be received, database and procedures that are required to convert the output from the input. Analysis phase is one of the very important phases for system development. In this phase, each detail is studied with a view to finding the exact solution. So, many things which are not indicated in the initiation/initial survey phase, come out at this stage. It is worthwhile to note that proposed solution may change once this phase is completed. This phase deals with more details as a foundation stage. All other steps are fully dependent on this phase. The developer or the analyst spends a lot of time in this phase. In addition, the cost benefit analysis prepared during the initiation/initial survey phase should also be reviewed for accuracy and cost and time estimates.

This is one of the complex phases for any large system development. Many information system specialists appreciate the difficulties of fully understanding the large, complex systems. One of the methods is the structured analysis method aimed at overcoming such difficulties. The basic concept is partitioning the system into components and constructing a model of the system. It narrows the communication gap between the users and the system analyst. It helps in carrying out the subsequent phase of structured designing. But it cannot accomplish how the application should be implemented. Rather, it allows the user to understand the logical elements apart from the physical components it uses.

One of the tools of structured analysis is the data flow diagram. **Data flow diagram** is a graphical documentation of the system. It describes a system to prepare a narrative outlining its features, describing how it interacts with other elements and identifying its function, etc. It is a top-down process. An initial overview model is exploded into more details. Each process can be broken down into a yet more detailed data flow diagram. This may occur repeatedly, to allow the analyst to fully understand the system. A data flow diagram uses the following four basic elements:

- External entity
- Data flow
- Process
- Data store

SPOTLIGHT

A customer can deposit and withdraw money from a bank branch. One has to fill a pay-in-slip to deposit money and enclose the cheque with it. The cheque amount is verified against the slip after which the customer's account is updated. The passbook of the account holder is also updated.

In Figure 9.2, the cube represents an external entity which is a source and/or destination of data. The circle represents a process where data are

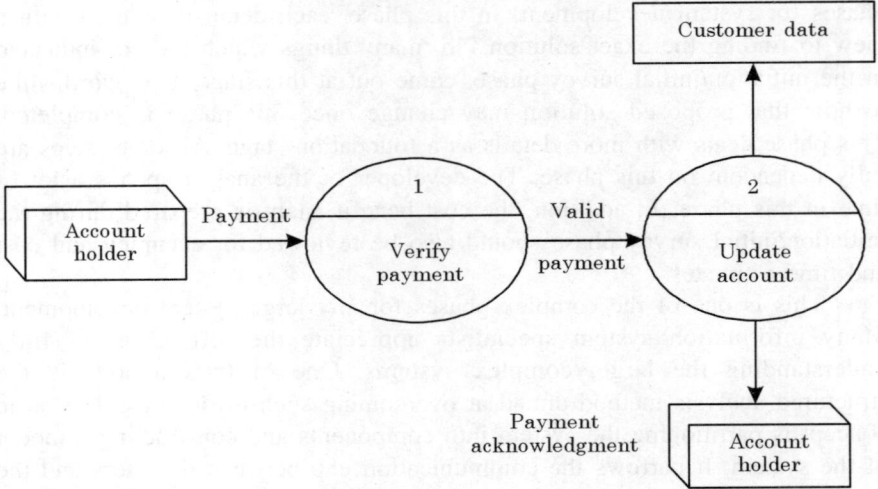

Figure 9.2 Data flow diagram.

transformed from one form to another. Basically, some amount of work is performed on data in any process. The arrow represents the data flow in the direction in which the data moves. The data flow names are written with the line. It is an interface between the different components of data flow diagram. Lastly, the open-ended rectangle represents the data store, which is repository of data.

The data flow diagram is one of the most useful tools for the analysis phase. It gives an overall picture to top-level management. It also helps the programmer for the future development of the system.

Design phase

The next phase is the design phase. Here the emphasis is changed—how the system will work, and whether the system will meet the requirement, etc. are identified during system analysis. The system design describes each input, output, operation and file. In this phase, the documents are fairly technical. The system analyst works out in detail the requirement of facilities, equipment and personnel. The manual procedures are prepared to operate the system. The documents containing the design specifications list the designs in various forms, charts, tables and special symbols. The detailed design information is passed on for programming. Control is an important aspect of the design. The analyst must assume that mistakes will be made while entering data or functions. Some mistakes are minor and inconsequential, but others can be so serious, and could lead to erasure of data or improper application of the system. The control provides ways to:

(1) validate the data for accuracy
(2) ensure that authorized users only access the system
(3) filter the necessary data.

A policy is prepared for all user-designed applications to review the system and assist in the development of the system. End-user development method is adopted by many analysts.

Construction phase

The construction phase includes:

(1) complete test of computer programs and instructions like user manual, software manual, etc.
(2) all tasks to carry out the conversion from old system to new system.
(3) installation of all software and hardware.

Implementation phase

In the implementation phase, system personnel install new hardware, train the users, install software and create files of data needed. The system developer may choose to pilot run the operation in any one area of the organization. Sometimes it is better to run the old and the new systems together to compare the efficiency and results. For small system development, the system developers prefer to install or implement the system as a whole. Each implementation strategy has its merits depending on the business situation in which it is involved. The developers strive to ensure that the system should be trouble free, regardless of the implementation strategy.

The application has to be maintained and changes will be made to software files and procedures to meet the emerging software requirements. In that sense, implementation is an ongoing process.

Maintenance phase

Maintenance is one of the major parts in the software development of an organization. The lifetime of any software product is fairly short. It is not possible for every organization to upgrade to the latest version of the existing product or switch to a new program. In such situations the analysis should begin with a determination of the system's value to the business. Having determined the value of the system, different options may be considered like restructuring, refreshing, rewriting and replacing, etc. But one can consider the following points before taking a decision:

(1) Programmer's experience with the existing program
(2) Adaptability of the existing program
(3) Moving to a new hardware base
(4) Availability of off-the-shelf replacement
(5) Transportability of the current system

Structured Analysis Development Method

One group of system analysts acknowledges the difficulty of understanding the large and complex systems in the organization. The Structured Analysis Method is aimed at overcoming such difficulties in the system through partitioning the system into components and constructing a model of the system. It does not state how the requirements would be accomplished or implemented. Structured Analysis Development Method focuses on what the system is required to do. It deals with the logical elements apart from the physical components of the system. It consists of elements requiring both analysis and design.

Essential elements of the Structured Analysis Development Method include the graphic symbols, data flow diagram and data dictionary. The Structured Analysis Development Method uses symbols or icons to represent a graphic model of the system. The data flow diagram is already discussed in the analysis phase of the System Development Life Cycle Method. Data dictionary consists of data flow, process and data stores. All definitions of elements are described in detail in a data dictionary.

Structured design is another element of the Structured Analysis Development Method that utilizes the graphic description. Structured design is a specific program design technique; it is not a comprehensive design method. The fundamental tool of structured design is the structure chart. The structure chart describes the interaction between the various modules. The Structured Analysis Development Method is often combined with the System Development Life Cycle Method described earlier.

System Prototype Method

The risk of a new system can be reduced somewhat by the technique of prototyping. A prototype model has some of the functions of the complete system. Use of prototype method leads to refinement, and the cycle is repeated. It helps the developer to improve the product through a repeat approach to the same module. The repetition helps in many ways to improve the quality of the product. This approach is favoured by those who view development as an evolutionary process. Figure 9.3 shows the evolutionary process of the prototype method.

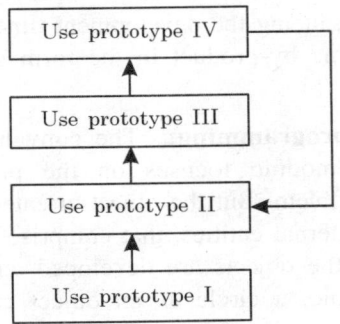

Figure 9.3 The prototype process.

A prototype model involves the users more directly than the System Development Life Cycle Method. In this model, the user can get a feel of what the system will look like and how it will function long before it is actually programmed and implemented. Normally it is possible to find out mistakes much earlier in the development process, saving substantial time and expenses at a later stage. The basic drawback is that poor system design may kill the whole objective. This can only be done if prototyping is employed at the right time and in the appropriate manner. The computer industry is pursuing application generator programs that generate other programs, to support prototyping effort.

The system development productivity can be enhanced through the choice of software and tools, even by delegating some subset of the development work to end-users. Over a period of time, this will be one of the tasks which allows the user the flexibility and ease of use. In a true sense, it is difficult to measure productivity of the development which is a much-debated task. Each of the following techniques has demonstrated a potential to facilitate some parts of the development activity.

Programming language: The fourth generation programming language has reduced the development time compared to the third generation language. This language helps the user to generate tailored reports or conduct specific inquiries, thus reducing some of the many routine demands placed on the system development group. The user friendliness of this language is based on the complexity; complicated and high volume programs usually consume more computer resources compared to third generation language. But in general, this may not hinder the user as computer processing speeds are increasing, and prices are dropping rapidly.

Computer aided software engineering (CASE): 'Computer-aided software engineering' is often described in terms of aids to system development and aids to system design. It provides a consistent system of support for all phases of system analysis and design from initial survey through conversion and testing. Besides improving the quality of the software products and reducing the development time, many CASE environments provide a welcome by-product in the form of improved, automatic documentation.

Object-oriented programming: The conventional approach to the development program module focuses on the processes that must be performed to solve a problem. But the object-oriented programming module reflects the object, or external entities, that comprise the problem. In object-oriented programming, the objects are developed and used in a variety of applications. For example, a circle as an object can be used to draw a circular field as a playground and it can be used as a ring of a cycle. The object-oriented modules are more readily generalized to other problems that involve similar type of objects. These modules are easier to understand and maintain.

9.3 MANAGING SYSTEM DEVELOPMENT PROCESS

The system development passes through different stages. Time and people are the two important factors of resources. The introduction of a new system always involves new ways for an organization to do its work. A number of factors have been found important in successful implementation of a new system. The most important is the support of management in implementing a new system. A key factor in software project overruns is the difficulty of accurately estimating time, effort and cost. It is important to develop strategy both prior to the start of a software project and also while it is under way. The System Development Life Cycle Method is an important management tool for monitoring a project. It is useful because each stage can serve as a check point for the project as a guide for formal reviews. It should be noted that the time in each stage may not be accurately reflected by considering only the person-months of effort. One of the common yardsticks in a software project is the efforts expended against progress. It signifies that persons and months are interchangeable and adding more person to a software project would decrease the time needed to complete it. But software development is a complex process where interrelationships—the need for communication is great—and the tasks cannot be neatly partitioned. As a result, adding more persons to a software project often lengthens the schedule.

There are several other factors which can contribute to a disaster:

(1) Projects are not defined or estimated adequately
(2) Invalid skill assumption is made
(3) Roles are not defined
(4) Project planning is ignored
(5) Project milestones are not defined. So, project reporting is trivial
(6) "Quality" is never defined

Normally in-house projects are developed by own programmers, analysts, etc. The organization invariably fails to focus on the software development process. Programmers are more keen to implement the software project even if the project needs much more time to accomplish the benefit. On the other hand, where the project is outsourced from a vendor, the vendor may fail to deliver the software product on time, because different types of interventions had occurred during the system development stages. In both these situations, one person or group of people should be responsible to implement the software project. All kinds of communications must pass through this person or group. This person or group should be capable enough to handle the software project.

In many cases, it is more cost effective to buy software rather than develop. System managers are often faced with a make-buy decision. The acquisition of software depends on the following factors:

(a) Software may be purchased or licensed
(b) Software may be acquired, then modified and integrated to meet specific needs
(c) Software may be custom-built by an outside developer

In some cases, it is better to purchase the less expensive software and experiment it to conduct a lengthy evaluation. For more expensive software products, estimate the internal cost of development and the date of completion. The selection of a software vendor is based on the company that meets the requirement specifications. It is recommended to develop a comparison matrix that presents a comparison of key functions. If possible, consult other users and seek their opinions. Support function is another issue in this case. The cost of outside support may be more than that of the inside. The trend towards outsourcing will continue for small and medium size companies.

REVIEW QUESTIONS

1. Discuss in detail the System Development Life Cycle (SDLC) method.
2. What are the differences between the logical design and the physical design?

3. What is a data flow diagram?
4. What do you understand by end-user development method?
5. What are the factors that need to be considered in the successful implementation of a new system?
6. What are the factors responsible for the failure of an information project?
7. What are the advantages of prototyping in any project?
8. Is management of information development different from management of other projects?
9. What are the basic functions of a system analyst?
10. What are the purposes of system development?

DISCUSSION QUESTIONS

1. Several different types of information systems exist in an organization. Give your own views on this statement.
2. The first thing we should decide is, whether we want to build or outsource an application. Give your opinion on this statement.

10

E-Commerce

10.1 FOUNDATION OF ELECTRONIC COMMERCE

The internet has fundamentally changed the world. There is no assumption or futuristic statement that we can all take for granted. The electronic commerce revolution has touched throughout the world. Electronic commerce has become a significant element for industry. Electronic commerce is a concept that describes the process of buying, selling and exchanging products, services and information through the internet. We know one can simply exchange information through e-mail services. Here from a communication perspective, the delivery of information is important. In the light of business, electronic commerce is the technology to automate a business process. The business community applies electronic commerce as a vehicle to run business. From an online concept, electronic commerce provides the capability of selling and buying products through the internet.

The effects of the Internet are, obviously not limited to corporations. In India, where computer has been growing rapidly, the internet users are still much less usage than those in other developed countries. On the other hand, the number of internet hosts has continued to grow at an impressive rate. Secondly, a variety of domains have experienced great growth. The internet society has started adding new domain names for more classification. The latency, total time taken for a piece of information to travel to a known destination and return, has improved a lot. The speed of data interchange has been improving very fast. In India, Videsh Sanchar Nigam Limited (VSNL) offers dial-up, ISDN and lease line services with good speed and infrastructure. Many villages have already been connected through the Internet. The story of e-choupal is the success story and is gaining rich experiences through time. The digitization is not possible in all areas of business in a traditional way. There are restrictions in electronic commerce too. For example, basically it is not possible to deliver the product over the counter; the payment in a currency form is not possible to be transferred. Finally, the role of an agent is not feasible in electronic commerce. Therefore, electronic commerce can take many forms depending on the product, the process and the agent or intermediary. A product can be physical or digital and it is also true for both process and agent. The combination represents pure electronic commerce or mixed condition. Thus, when all three are digital, it represents pure electronic commerce, i.e. digital product, digital agent and digital process. In all other cases, it is a mix of physical and digital dimensions.

A common classification of electronic commerce is by the type and the nature of the transaction. All electronic commerce business can be placed into two categories—pure plays and brick-and-clicks. Here pure play means, online purchases only. On the other hand, brick-and-click business combines physical presence with online presence.

SPOTLIGHT

> The amazon.com and bn.com (Barnes and Noble) are online book sellers, whereas Barnes and Noble has its own bookstore as well. When a customer buys a book from amazon.com, he pays by credit card. The product is delivered at the customer's premises. On the other hand, at Barnes and Nobles the customer has the choice to select a book from the site or search in the stores of Barnes and Noble. Thus, the customer can also buy the book from the bookstore itself. In case of amazon.com, except for the delivery process and agent, the book store is a virtual one. Pure play business uses the capability of Internet.

Business can be classified on the basis of the types of the buyers and sellers.

Business-to-Consumer (B2C)

This is a retailing transaction with the individual. There can be direct sellers, intermediaries, advertising-based models, fee-based models, etc. In direct sellers, one kind is the seller entailers. They do not manufacture, but collect the orders from the consumers and either directly ship the products or pass the order on to vendor for delivery. It has also become possible to have direct contact with the customers. For example, amazon.com is selling books, CDs, etc. In India, rediff.co.in, ebay.co.in and yahoo.co.in are in the B2C category.

Building traffic continues to be the biggest challenge faced faced by the B2C sites. It is a very difficult job to sustain customer loyalty. Online customers are very price sensitive and can be easily lured away.

Business-to-Business (B2B)

Most of the electronic commerce today is of the B2B type. The business is restricted to two entities which follow the same characteristics:

- High value of purchase
- Large order size
- Items purchased
- Buying centre-specific
- Special service available, etc.

In India, B2B market place has huge potential. Today, many companies are offering services through their own sites. For example, customers can buy products from ril.com (Reliance Industries Ltd.), tatasteel.com (Tata Steel Ltd.).

Consumer-to-Consumer (C2C)

Here one consumer sells directly to other consumers. Some auction sites offer C2C services. In India, C2C may be successful in the long run.

Business-to-Government (B2G)

In this category, government buys from business houses. It is one of the vast areas and has lot of potential in the future. Many state governments in India have started e-governance projects in their various departments.

Non-business electronic commerce

Many non-government organizations, not-for-profit organizations and religious organizations are using electronic commerce to reduce their expenses or to improve their efficiency.

Electronic commerce is an innovation in global economics. The technology, low cost, anywhere-anyone, variety of possibilities and rapid growth of infrastructure resulted in potential benefits to the organization, society and consumers. These benefits will increase four-fold as electronic commerce expands.

Benefits of electronic commerce to **organizations** or **firms** are as given below:

(a) There is no boundary for this market as well as there is nothing to store.
(b) The electronic procurement can reduce the purchase cost.
(c) It is possible to sell special kind of products such as old coins, furniture, etc.
(d) It is possible to customize products and services.

Benefits of electronic commerce to **consumers** are listed below:

(a) It enables to shop 24 hours and 365 days in any location.
(b) As sellers save substantial amount from the business, the partial benefit goes to the consumers. As a result, the cost of the product is reduced or more discounts are offered.
(c) Customers have more choices, they can choose products as well as vendors.
(d) Relevant information is available once the transaction is completed. It saves time as well as money.

Benefits of electronic commerce to **society** are given below:

(a) As the Internet is within the reach of anybody, even less affluent people can buy on the Internet.
(b) The public services such as health, education, and social services can be distributed at a reduced cost. As a result, the cost of the product is reduced or more discounts are offered.
(c) It allows individual to work at home, resulting in less traffic and lower air pollution.
(d) The savings from electronic commerce help individual in saving and spending more which contribute to the economic exchequer.

We will now discuss the **driving forces** and **limitations** of electronic commerce.

The communication technology has not yet fully improved in most of the places. The security and reliability are the major areas of concern. Payment system in electronic commerce is still not acceptable to consumers. Customers do not trust an unknown, faceless vendor. Legal issue is one of the stumbling blocks to electronic commerce. Many legal issues, government regulations and standards are not refined enough. The computer penetration is very low in India compared to other developing countries.

The main **driving forces** in electronic commerce are business pressure and global economy. The competition has changed the nature of business. Organizations are adopting different tools or vehicles, which act as competitive advantage. Other reasons are government deregulations, political changes, low labour cost in some countries, information overload and technological obsolescence.

Electronic commerce with all kinds of **limitations** is still a new area. More people are joining this area everyday and creating more and more websites. The electronic commerce market should be understood at various levels, i.e. from the managerial, historical, technical and customer perspectives.

10.2 RETAILING

Electronic retailer is one kind of business community in electronic commerce business. The company must understand the profit orientation of the virtual market. One of the objectives of the business is to maximize the shareholder value through the maximization of value of the customer. Electronic retailers have developed some business models to achieve those goals. As discussed earlier, an organization may have purely online business or electronic business along with traditional business. It is interesting to note that online business is quite different from the traditional business. The success stories may be different for both, but the nature of the business model is important to us.

Firstly, the business must be clearly defined, what proportion of its business will be online and how this might change over time. It is more important to know how the product proportion will change over time in retail business. Many organizations start their business with one kind of product like toys, books, cassettes or kitchenwares. But later, most of them start selling combinations of products.

Secondly, business must understand the revenue part and the purpose of the online business. It may be a cost centre as well. Today most of the companies listed in stock exchange, have their own websites. Many companies allow their customers to buy products from their own sites. Initially, they may start with loss-centre, keeping in mind the long-term business objective.

Thirdly, the selection of the target customer is an important task, in terms of behaviour (e.g. surfing pattern, buying pattern, time consciousness); demographics (e.g. age, sex, income); psychographics (e.g. lifestyle, value). Once those things are developed, the business must try to clarify the way for maximizing customer value. Revenue generation is the major area of concern in electronic retailing business.

Normally the business on online is conducted in the following ways:

(1) **Commerce:** Selling products or services to consumer.

(2) **Advertising:** Selling advertising space to interested advertisers.

(3) **Fees:** Charging fees for special services, like home delivery, information on other company's product, etc.

(4) **Commission:** Charging commission from credit card agency, courier service agency, etc.

Retailing in India is in the preliminary stage. Retailing is more organized in metro and big cities. But the local grocery shop is the real area for retailing business. The direct-to-home market is also being run well. By using internet, manufacturers can directly contact customers. The manufacturers' direct marketing can be successful, as long as they sell established brands and their sites are well known to the consumers. Therefore, the site itself plays a major role in internet retailing business. It is also possible to display more and more catalogues to attract customers to the physical stores.

Before we proceed further, let us review some retail products in electronic market. The electronic market in retailing has been expanding very fast. In this embryonic stage of electronic commerce, it is very difficult to predict the sale volume. The major items sold are gifts, books, foods, apparels and accessories, music, videos, toys, consumer finance, insurance, etc.

SPOTLIGHT

Companies are selling different products starting from mobile phones to television sets on websites like retailers. Products are displayed on the website giving the details of the product. Products are listed under different categories like home appliances, kitchen appliances, etc. A customer can choose a product from different categories available on the site. Search engine support is also available where the product may not be on display on the website. A consumer can find out the product with the help of a search engine. Payments are made in advance in any mode like demand draft or cash or by credit card. The products are delivered through courier services to the customer. ebay.in is one website which offers both buying and selling of products. In ebay.in, consumers are registered to buy and sell the product and they input all information like address of delivery, mode of payment, credit card details, etc. They can sell used products also through the website. Many products are listed with price on the home page, where a customer can choose the product. The search engine allows the customer to search for a product. Details of the product with selling price is available to the consumer. On the other hand, a seller lists products for selling on the site. A seller has many choices in the case of buying the product from the website with lowest price range available. The seller can reach anyone interested in the product. The ebay receives commission from both the buyer and the seller. They do not have any stores for storing the products that are displayed on the website. It is possible to display any number of products on a website without any additional cost.

The vendors have adopted different models depending on their nature of products. Direct marketing is one of the tools. Here no intermediaries are involved. The manufacturer advertises and distributes products to customers, via electronic store on the internet. Dell computer launched online sales and services through internet at www.dell.com in July 1996.

All the items, desktops, workstations, note books, servers are available through internet. Anyone can buy products from any location. It offers to customize products through their own websites. In India, products can be purchased from ril.com (Reliance Industries Ltd.), tatasteel.com (Tata Steel Ltd.). The major breakthrough comes from price competitiveness owing to mass customization. Secondly, service is available at a single contact point to the whole world. Delivery support is another issue in selling products through internet. Basic costs include maintenance of home page, network operation, merchandising and collection of payment.

Electronic intermediaries can be classified as pure or partial, depending upon the level of commitment to the electronic retailing business. In the first case, the organization sells products manufactured by others. The amazon.com has been selling books through internet. It has listed about 10 million titles in its electronic catalogue, although it actually keeps an inventory of only thousand files in its own warehouse. FedEx delivers the merchandise to customers. On the other hand, the order goes to owner's site and they direct the order to producer's site. Business houses have opened online department stores worldwide. The cyber customers may be familiar with some sites for buying products. The difficulties such as how to access the price or product features offered by other retail online stores may arise. Search engines may help us to find out the same product on different websites. The capability required to search for goods on hundreds of websites in consonance with time puts unprecedented pressure on web retailers. The definition of the term 'comparable' may be different for each consumer. There are many software agents available for the comparison of products. They help users to find products that they are likely to enjoy. It uses information gathered from others, similar to user's tastes and opinions, to suggest a new product. In computer related shopping, comparison is available on many sites. The compare.net is one of the sites which supports retrieval of comparable items. Software agents like jango.com, junglee.com, mysimon.com etc. can find products and compare their prices. For example, netbuyer.com helps to purchase computer and communication products. The method of comparison starts with search, and the next step supports the elimination of options. The third step is to solve criteria in terms of price, specifications and delivery time, etc. The online retailing business via internet has given birth to new kind of intermediaries. The manufacturers can sell directly to customers and service their products online. So, the traditional intermediaries like dealers, wholesalers, etc. are eliminated. This phenomenon is called dis-intermediation. However, new kind of intermediaries like e-brokers are emerging. This phenomenon can be known as re-intermediation. But the traditional business distribution system, payment system, etc. have changed to provide something that the electronic business system cannot do. Even the market is self-driven. If we consider the situation, where the number of sellers and buyers are not under control, the basic question is how to differentiate between those sellers, whose deliverables look the same. The answer may be difficult as customers are in the process of learning. It is more important for a seller to help the customers in the learning process and update them continuously. Business houses have to investigate before starting a completely new business in order to cultivate the future opportunity for retailing in electronic commerce.

10.3 SERVICE INDUSTRY

The electronic commerce has taken over most of the service-related business.

It may be banking, travel and tourism industry, stock broking, insurance, magazines and journals. Let us start with a very simple example of mailing service. In past, most business organizations were used to spend more than fifty hours a month for posting and mailing of business-related documents. If we add in-house distribution of documents, it will simply double the amount of time spent on this delivery and distribution system. The e-mail, a paid service, has saved a substantial amount of time and money.

> **SPOTLIGHT**
>
> The traditional library of any university or school orders periodicals regularly. The process starts with contacting an agent to place the order. The agent, who is in contact with a number of publishers places orders. The average time to deliver a domestic periodical is three days, whereas for an international, it is not less than one week. The process is slow and expensive for the library, which pays commission to the agent and also loses discount which the publisher passes on to the agent.

In travel and tourism industry, a sea change has taken place throughout the world. A traveller basically looks for information like details of the places he likes to travel, hotels, different rates and tariffs of services offered, weather details if possible, communication details, etc. Today he can log on to any site relating to travel industry and gather any information at any time. Those sites offer a lot of additional services like ticket booking, tour planning, accommodation planning on behalf of the customer. One should not compare the efforts required to plan a tour in the traditional way with those involved in electronic commerce. In the traditional way, travel agents help clients to take decisions. However, in online travel business, customers are equipped with more information to take the decisions themselves.

The job market is one of the largest markets in the world where employees are looking for a job. A selection and the recruitment process is one of the major functional areas for any organization. The employers can save substantial amount of time and money with the help of the selection process through the internet.

In all the cases discussed above, different types of business models are followed. A systematic approach to identify the architecture for business models can be based on value chain deconstruction and reconstruction. This is to identify value chain elements and integrate information along the chain. Here, the value change reconstruction means identifying the elements such as inbound logistic operations, marketing and sales, technology development and human resource management. The basic difference compared with the manufacturing industry is that the service can be produced at the time of delivery. When we deal with a pure electronic commerce system, which is possible in a service industry, the potential advantages are the greatest, since the automation of the entire process can result in a substantial cost reduction.

As more and more people start using electronic commerce in the service industry, different types of agencies will probably vanish, as their jobs will increasingly get replaced by technology.

The travel industry is expanding throughout the world. Any experienced traveller knows that he can save a considerable amount of money and time by good planning. As discussed earlier, the internet is the ideal place to plan, explore and arrange almost any trip to anywhere in the world. The benefits to travellers are enormous—free information, discounts and hassle-free service. The sites dealing with travel industry provide the facilities listed below:

(a) Personalized service with the help of the multimedia presentation via internet
(b) Low cost trips
(c) Paperless environment
(d) 24×7 environment
(e) Information available at home

Online travel however has also its own **limitations**. They are as follows:

(a) Many people do not have the access to the internet.
(b) The amount of time and difficulties of using virtual travel information is another area of concern.
(c) Typical tour programmes require specialized knowledge and arrangements, where the travel agent plays a major role. Therefore, business houses which opt for this require collaborative approach for successful implementation of their strategy.

Banking and financial services have developed a lot of expertise in the area of electronic commerce. Today the location of a bank does not affect a customer's choice. Electronic banking or cyber banking has capabilities ranging from paying bills to securing loans electronically. Banks have its own websites. A customer can get account balance at any time from his residence or office. He can pay bills of utility services like telephone bill, electricity bill, etc., sitting at home. It is easy to take printout of any statement available by sending mail to the bank.

Electronic banking offers enormous advantages to the banks and their customers, such as expanding the customer base and saving the cost of other transactions. Corporate houses have started using internet banking services. Business houses can pay for mortgage, effect automatic transfer of funds to other account of the company, and pay the customer directly, etc. The updated account information plays a vital role in decision-making. Electronic banking system through internet has changed the functions dramatically. In India, HDFC Bank, ICICI, Standard Chartered Bank, HSBC, UTI Bank, etc. offer internet banking.

On the other side, an electronic commerce organization must have one bank for transactions. Therefore, it is mandatory for a bank to be the part of the electronic commerce.

Since the inception of the internet, the job market has been mostly transferred to it. It has many **advantages** as follows:

(a) Cost of newspaper advertisement is expensive.
(b) Normally the life cycle of the advertisement on the internet is days or weeks. The organization has its own websites with career options. So anyone can look for an employment opportunity. At the same time, the database is also developed for future employees.
(c) Nation-wide advertisements are expensive. Place is not a constraint at all for internet advertising.
(d) It is much more easy to find a job on the internet via search engines or other processes.
(e) Some applications or letters of response tend to get lost or arrive late. This chance factor is eliminated on the internet.

Internet offers a perfect environment for employers who otherwise have to work hard to find employees.

Internet has given birth to a new type of intermediary in job market. They have their own websites with information about the job market. They offer free personality test, interview preparation, career guidance, job interview, etc. They also offer a very specialized service, where the employee and the employers can update themselves with the latest information. For example, a person can register by listing the details of career like the area of interest, location preferred, salary level, etc. The personal e-mail account of the registered person is updated daily or weekly based on the information provided by him. He is kept informed continuously about the opportunities.

Many other services are available on the internet. Online publishing is electronic delivery of journals, magazines through internet. Emerland, a leading distributor of journals allow customers to download journals and magazines. The service is available instantly at any time. Subscribers can pay one-time cost a year or pay whenever convenient. This is one of the examples of pure electronic commerce, i.e. digital product, digital agent and digital process. Auctions, an established method of commerce for generations, deal with products and services for which conventional marketing methods are not sufficient. There are several types of auctions available on the internet. The methods are also different. Most auctions open to the public. Items auctioned frequently are computers, art works, antiques, rare coins, airline tickets and many other products. Today insurance, health care, matchmaking, electronic stamps are also available as other online services.

10.4 MARKET RESEARCH

The most difficult task for any company is to acquire and to retain a large customer base. Getting customer information and marketing information is one of the company's biggest problems. Basically the company gathers information from distributors, retailers but formal market research is expensive. **Market research** is concerned with finding information about consumers, products, marketing methods and marketers. It helps to identify marketing opportunities and issues to develop strategy. Market research is also a methodical way to gather information about topics such as the industry, economy, product, price, distributor promotion and consumer behaviour. Basically, market research is process oriented. It follows several different stages enumerated below:

(a) Research objective and problem
(b) Data collection
(c) Data analysis
(d) Recommendations
(e) Implementation

Companies communicate with consumers in many ways—television advertisements, radio, direct mails, newspapers, websites and banner advertisements. The internet is a media of communication that must work with all other media to communicate consistent messages. Electronic commerce is one of the media, which helps organizations to conduct market research online. It is a powerful tool for conducting market research on consumer behaviour, identifying new markets, and new product developments, etc. The consumers in the internet are of different kinds compared to the traditional market. There are many aspects that are the part of the market research in marketing. In this topic, our interest is on conducting market research through internet. It is possible by mailing all registered users. Internet-based market research is often done in an interactive mode, even in a multimedia format. The main difficulty is the inaccurate information provided by the users. But it is possible to learn about customers by observing other factors rather than interacting with them. Many marketers keep track of consumers' web movements by using cookie files attached to a users' browser to help in tracking the web surfers' movements online. Hence, internet offers is a very strong ground for market research. It is very easy to incorporate radio buttons, data entry fields, and check boxes in the questionnaire. Data entry boxes are filled with many answers, which keep respondents from selecting choice or adding comments, where none was intended. It is also possible to force respondents to fill information that is mandatory in nature and then allow him or her to proceed for the next answer. Responses can be validated as entered and other elements can be added, such as graphics, logos, etc. In many cases, it is possible to link other websites for more information to be filled in. In addition, respondents have the flexibility of responding in their own time, at their own place.

When an interview is done through internet and e-mail, the cost part becomes minimum, because respondents spend their own time and cost to participate in market research.

On the flip side, the consumers have to have access to the internet. Long download times and slow processing may lead to frustration on the part of the respondent. Further, online research is not suitable for every client or product. Although the web users' demographic pattern is rapidly expanding, it is still in the hands of the younger people. Online research is not suitable for manufacturing companies, as it may not sufficiently reach their target markets.

Online market research will soon change the relationship between the retailers and the consumers. It provides an opportunity to be in more close and deeper relationship with consumers. As a result, it helps tracking purchase and preference data and analysing the information to predict the products and services which the customer may need. It has potential to capture customers for new products and services.

10.5 ELECTRONIC COMMERCE STRATEGY AND IMPLEMENTATION

In more recent times, the world has seen the rise and the fall of the dot-com companies mainly serving the B2C market. The lists are many throughout the world. The venture capitalists have burnt their fingers in internet-based business. The consensus is that they did not follow the basic principles and practices of business. They build their market with zero pricing and free service. As a result, the customers were not loyal and visited casually out of curiosity. The customer data was incomplete or wrong in most of the cases. Registration of a website or completing a form online does not equate to a strong relationship. Most of them underestimate the human behaviour, while proposing new business models, new ways of shopping and many new ways of doing things via internet. It was not an easy task to change customers' habits and shopping behaviour. Many dot-coms had a grandiose vision of building a world market place but flopped against the established business relations matured over several years. As a result, they changed and adopted the market downturn. Fifty per cent of B2C companies shifted to the B2B model. Many of them adopted new business models to upstream customers. New kinds of services were offered in addition to the online service.

Thus strategy is the issue for any business, so it is also true for electronic commerce business. After the dot-com crash, the internet is growing at a steady pace. The number of internet hosts has been growing at an impressive rate. Strategy formulations could include many issues and long discussions. Here, we will only focus on some major issues and their implementation strategies.

The value analysis approach is one strategy on the internet. Value to a consumer is his perception of the consequences of using a product or services in relation to prior expectations. Consumers commonly make value judgments in relation to price. Several factors as follows need to be analyzed to develop a strategy.

(a) Specific product or service
(b) Target audience
(c) Technical infrastructure
(d) Competitive analysis
(e) Financial functioning
(f) Demographic information
(g) Promotion and internal connection

This strategy formulation is done under the support of top-level management. Each area is analyzed in detail and key success factors are identified. The business models are developed to implement strategy. The revenue model, marketing model, logistic model and payment system are developed under the business model. Technology and site are the important areas of concern. The development of a website should focus on all strategic areas of concern because different models are interconnected and needed to be controlled.

Strategy needs an implementation plan too. The implementation plan outlines the steps to follow during implementation. Implementation may also be done through two ways. In the first case, a pilot project can be tested and implemented. Implementation as a whole requires substantial investment in infrastructure. Thus once the pilot project is successful, the company may go ahead with the remaining issues, being also a part of planning. It is better to implement services in the beginning to gain confidence of the consumers. A company can allocate functional jobs such as outsourcing, supply chain, etc. to different web teams. Intermediaries are developed under each functional area and project. A project leader is selected to integrate all those areas under the website.

Web content design is another important area, which is developed under a project leader. The security and control of web contents are important factors that must be considered throughout the developing process.

Project assessment is also a part of the implementation process. The project should deliver what it is supposed to perform. The organization should start identifying failing projects as soon as possible and should trace out the reasons behind the failures. The organization should reassess the strategy in order to learn from failures in order to improve or to change future planning.

The internet is no longer a free bird. It is still true that "the internet changes everything." Compare the world ten years ago with the present world and spot the myriad differences the internet has already made.

REVIEW QUESTIONS

1. Describe the major characteristics of electronic commerce.
2. Explain how electronic commerce can reduce the cycle time of a product or service.
3. How can electronic commerce facilitate customization of products and services?
4. Define electronic commerce and electronic business.
5. Define intranet and extranet.
6. Describe the process of internet shopping.
7. How can a product be (price) competitive in electronic commerce market?
8. Define the agent-based services with examples.
9. What do you understand by online publishing?
10. What are the major benefits of trading online?
11. Explain the goals of a market research in electronic commerce market.
12. What are the major methods of internet-based market research?
13. Describe the profile of an internet user?
14. How does electronic commerce affect organizations?

DISCUSSION QUESTIONS

1. What are the critical success factors in e-commerce for retaining customers' loyalty?
2. An intelligent agent plays a vital role in online travel. Discuss this statement with examples.
3. The future of banking is through internet. Give your views with examples.
4. The online employment service makes it easy to change jobs. What can companies do to overcome this problem?

11
Supply Chain Management

11.1 COMPETITIVE ADVANTAGE OF SUPPLY CHAIN MANAGEMENT

Organizations exist to maximize the value of the stockholders which, in turn, means maximization of value to the customer. The driving force for every business is to increase value to the customer. Products have their own dimensions and nature. The consumers also have different types of expectations from the company. It has long been an axiom in marketing that the customer is attracted by benefits and not necessarily by the product. A product is purchased not for itself but what it will deliver to the customer. Let us look at the product milk that is supplied every morning to customers in packets or take the example of the newspaper delivered every morning at the customers' doorsteps. In the first case, milk is produced, packed and distributed all over the city by vans. In the second case, newspapers are printed and then distributed through agents, local agents and delivery boys (Figure 11.1).

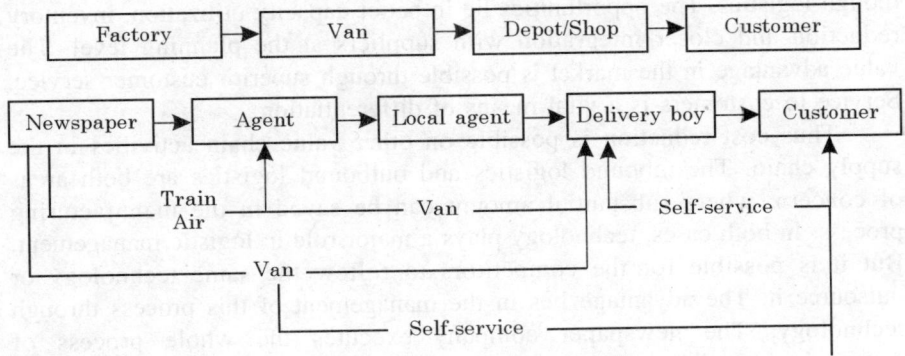

Figure 11.1 Distribution process.

In each case how the customer values the product is of great importance to the organization. This is nothing but managing the supply of products to the customers. Managing the whole process of distribution can be defined as **Supply Chain Management (SCM)**. There are many ways of defining the supply chain but the concept can be better elucidated as follows:

Supply chain management is a process of managing the movement and storage of materials, purchase functions and finished good inventory, through the organization and its marketing channels, in such a way which maximizes the profit through cost-effective fulfilment of orders. There are three flows within any chain—physical goods, money and information.

The business consists of 'three Cs'. The 'three Cs' in question are the *customers*, the *competition* and the *company*. The ability of the company to be competitive lies in differentiating itself in the eyes of the customers. This is possible through cost advantage or value advantage or ideally both. The productivity advantage gives a lower cost profile and the value advantage provides a differential 'plus' over a competitor's offerings.

Cost leadership strategies are based upon the volume maximization through economies of scale. The cost advantage comes not necessarily through economies of scale but through SCM. In many industries, the logistic cost represents a significant proportion of the total cost of the product and it is possible to achieve cost reduction through SCM. Supply Chain Management has the potential to assist the organization in achieving not only the cost and productivity advantage but also the value advantage.

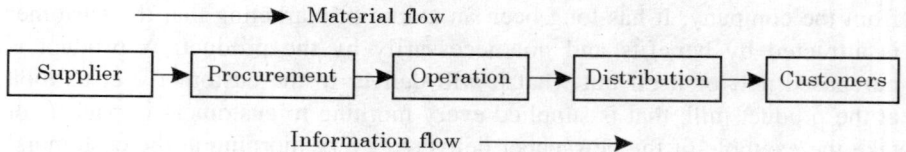

Figure 11.2 Flow process.

There are number of ways in which productivity can be enhanced though logistics. The opportunities lie in better capacity utilization, inventory reduction and closer integration with suppliers at the planning level. The value advantage in the market is possible through superior customer service. Service to customers is a vital means of differentiation.

Thus cost reduction is possible on other value chain activities in the supply chain. The inbound logistics and outbound logistics are both areas of concern, where substantial amount can be saved in the manufacturing process. In both cases, technology plays a major role in logistic management. But it is possible for the competitors to follow the same technology or outsource it. The advantage lies in the management of this process through technology. The newspaper company executes the whole process of distribution via different partners, like agents, subagents, etc. On the other hand, a manufacturer may not involve itself with all levels of intermediaries but each of them is linked till the process ends with the customer. As a result, a network is developed with different organizations that are involved, through upstream and downstream linkages.

In the case of raw materials, outsourcing is a buzzword throughout the world and companies only assemble the finished products on shop-floor. This trend has a long implementation period in logistic management. The challenges lie in integrating and coordinating the flow of materials from a multitude of suppliers, often offshore and managing the distribution of the finished products.

Thus the focus of SCM is in another way on management of relationships in order to achieve a more profitable outcome for all partners in the value chain. The chain is driven by market forces to achieve those competitive advantages. It could be termed demand chain management. The word 'chain' can be replaced by 'network', being a combination of suppliers, intermediaries, and customers.

11.2 MANAGING SUPPLY CHAIN MANAGEMENT

One of the most valuable resources within a supply chain is information. The time to launch a project starts with the orders being placed for raw materials on suppliers. The production issues the requisitions to stores or coordination department for raw materials.

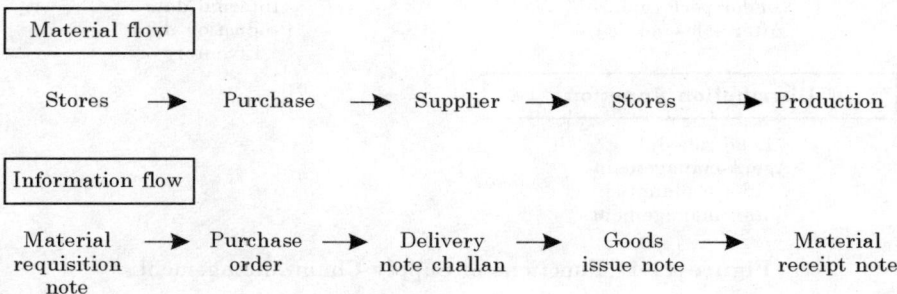

Figure 11.3 Flow of material and information in production.

The process described above is a general manufacturing process for inbound logistics. The delivery of goods starts from here. The product reaches ultimately to the customer. If we take into consideration that the material flow is not disturbed under any circumstances, then information flow is important. On the other hand, wrong information flow will hamper the whole process. The organization faces different types of problems on account of this flow disruption. So, this is nothing but managing the supply chain in the organization.

The major barrier to the implementation of the logistics concept is organizational. There is a great danger for those companies who do not recognize the need for organizational changes. The process is divided into different functions.

Figure 11.4 lists the major areas under Supply Chain Management. Individual functions are encouraged to optimize their own cost. The costing is done in individual functional areas. This is basically an activity-based costing. In reviewing the existing system, each element and link in the chain is examined to eliminate the 'non-value-added' activities. For example, paper work in many cases, in stores, warehouse, shop-floor is possible to be eliminated. Next to it is to develop the cross-functional team to develop the order fulfilment concept. The job rotation concept has been accepted by many organizations today. Organizations should focus on core areas for competency and out-source everything else. The only way by which significant development can be achieved is through top-level leadership.

Planning Function	Contact Function
Demand forecasting Strategy planning Stock management by product/customer	Production scheduling Material requirement planning Sales/Marketing planning

Control Function	Database Function
System performance External data Vendor performance After-sales service	Inbound shipments Customer order Internal data Production data Inventory

Distribution Function
Load scheduling Agent management Vehicle planning Retail management

Figure 11.4 Functions of Supply Chain Management.

Now in developing and implementing SCM, information technology has been playing the key role. Information systems are re-shaping the systems of the organization. Enterprise Resource Planning (ERP) is one of the solutions that links operations of the business, such as production and distribution, with supplier on the one hand and the customer on the other. Initially, it started with material resource planning. Later, manufacturing, distribution, and all other functions have been added to it. Information system is now the driving force for SCM. Supply chain integrates all processes upstream and downstream. By this collaborative working, the suppliers are also empowered by the common system and the shared information. The impetus for change may differ in companies but the direction of change has been the same. The system has the potential to convert the supply chain to demand chain. The system can respond to the known demand rather than to forecasting. The inventory is centralized and decisions pertaining to replenishment and orders are taken from one location. The database is centralized. Once the material is received by stores, the accounts department shares the same data for payment to the supplier. The same data is shared by the production department on the shop-floor. Marketing department has access to finished goods data, developed by production. The same data is shared by distribution for load sharing, vehicle management. The synchronized supply chain represents the final step in the evolution. At each stage, time is saved. As data entered once is used by the first user, reports are generated while the data is being updated by the next user of that database.

Internet technology has added more value to SCM. The production database can be accessed by the suppliers from their computers through intranet and who can then update ready-to-supply raw material information. So the supplier is in a position to distribute the total finished goods to all his customers by running full capacity. One way that he can save the manufacturing cost is by full capacity utilization with no idle stock. It helps him save a substantial amount and pass the benefit to the manufacturers. On the other hand, manufacturers can allow other suppliers to access their website and update information online. The manufacturers can select the lowest priced supplier for raw materials.

On the other hand, retailers are authorized to input their demand through intranet on the company's website. The total demand is available in one single database. The distribution of the products is done as per demand data and the customer data is also updated.

The goal is not just information sharing, but also to synchronize operations. This type of supply chain allows a company's operations to be visible to its suppliers and partners. So, synchronization is possible as there is a seamless transfer of information and products. In these supply chains, the partners participate jointly and share decision-making, rather than one company dictating to others.

The supply chain management is a joint effort for partners linked with the process. Training is required for the employees of the organization and partners. The cost of technology is also shared by the company with partners. The partners and intermediaries are empowered for successful implementation of supply chain management.

11.3 SUPPLY CHAIN: VALUE ENGINEERING

So far we have discussed supply chain. The process is discussed in detail to understand the underlying mechanism. In each functional area, value engineering is possible, which contributes to SCM. But value engineering is not possible in the same way for all kinds of products.

Time is of essence in SCM. In manufacturing, internal customers are more important.

SPOTLIGHT

In a factory manufacturing industrial valves, the finished product from the foundry is the raw material for machine shop. The material is delivered to the customer from the machine shop as a finished product. Delay in foundry to deliver to shop-floor ends with a dissatisfied shop-floor employee who, in turn, is an internal customer. So, the delay in delivery to the customer implies a customer service penalty. The cost also increases as the inventory goes up. The holding cost of inventory increases the interest on working capital.

In this example, the manufacturing process can be streamlined through value engineering in functional areas such as manufacturing, forecasting for production and warehouse distribution. Information technology plays a very vital role in the value engineering process. Information is the key to the success of SCM process and for taking decisions. The lead time depends on supplier information, manufacturing information and demand information. Forecasting and distribution are dependent on retailing information with historical data. Information technology system can be segmented according to the stages of the supply chain. Legacy system is started with mainframe technology. Material planning system was implemented and later changed to enterprise resource planning. The latest addition is internet to manage communication supply chain.

Figure 11.5 shows an application map of supply chain. It has two parts, one with Enterprise Resource Planning with related software and the second part is internet with electronic commerce. ERP's advantage is the broad scope that it provides to analytical applications. Analytical systems are focused on critical function applications like planning and strategic decisions. Retails and distributions are connected through Sales Force Automation (SFA) systems. On the other hand, Supplier Management System (SMS) is a software which connects manufacturers with suppliers. The supply chain also includes demand planning and revenue management through ERP. In total, the application map consists of other functions as well, each backed with software. On the other side, the internet is the back bone. In the value chain, customers are managed through electronic commerce software, internal customers via intranet and ERP. The basic change is that the cost has come down substantially in the second case because communication is not only less costly but also fast. Thus, the value engineering in different stages as discussed earlier can increase the productivity of supply function with the help of information technology.

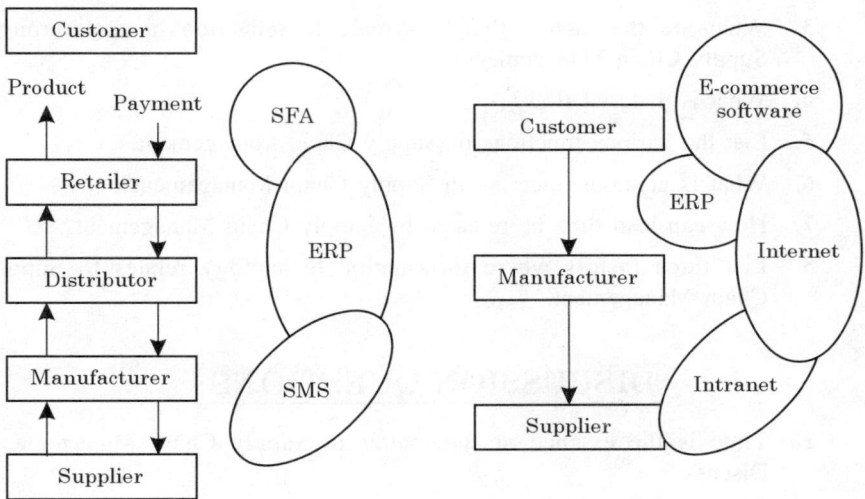

Figure 11.5 Application map of supply chain.

SPOTLIGHT

A doll manufacturing company sells its products to distributors. Distributors, in turn, reach out to customers via retailers. The company has no control on retailers as it needs substantial amount of investment to handle this process. The company distributes through vans to distributors and maintains reports with the help of supply chain software. The process takes at least one week to update the whole cycle from production to distribution. The company has recently implemented the internet-based software, which allows distributors to update the sales data daily. In addition to that, retailers can order via the internet. The whole process has shortened the distribution time to two days.

The supply chain software companies are realising that distribution management is to hold the key to B2B electronic exchange. They have also started their own exchanges by partnering with B2B exchanges. This has been creating a convergence of the supply chain companies and B2B exchanges. As a result, it creates a whole new set of opportunities for supply chain software developers. It also brings new competitors into the SCM landscape.

REVIEW QUESTIONS

1. What do you understand by Supply Chain Management?
2. How can productivity be enhanced through logistics?

3. What are the factors that contribute to reduction in cost through Supply Chain Management?
4. What is material flow?
5. List the various functions of Supply Chain Management.
6. What is value engineering in Supply Chain Management?
7. How can lead time be reduced by Supply Chain Management?
8. List three factors where information technology relates to Supply Chain Management.

DISCUSSION QUESTIONS

1. Time is the essence of the matter in Supply Chain Management. Discuss.
2. ERP or Enterprise Resource Planning has changed Supply Chain Management in manufacturing industries. Give your views.
3. Value engineering is a process under Supply Chain Management. Discuss.

12
Customer Relationship Management (CRM)

12.1 CUSTOMER RELATIONSHIP MANAGEMENT—A FRAMEWORK

Relationships have been studied by sociologists, social psychologists, anthropologists, philosophers and many other people. The traders and the businessmen have been relying on relationships for their success. In the early 1990s, the concept of relationships marketing was introduced formally. The service industry realised that the relationship marketing is the key term for their success. So, financial service institutions, airlines and other service providers found it more difficult to retain customers and reward the existing customers rather than running after new customers. They realized that building closer relationship with customers resulted in better returns to companies. Relationship marketing increases the use of company services by loyal customers. It is possible to charge premium price for customized product and services. Finally, satisfied customers generate more customers by referrals.

The concept of relationship marketing has also found application in the case of consumer products as well as industrial products. It is all about building relationship with customers which is the main objective of customer relationship management.

Relationships do not form overnight. Behavioural scientists commonly use the six-stage model to develop the relationship. The six stages are as follows:

1. Contact
2. Involvement

3. Intimacy
4. Deterioration
5. Repair
6. Dissolution

Basically, Customer Relationship Management (CRM) revolves around the customer life cycle management. It may be possible to develop a model that defines different stages in a relationship. A number of studies have looked at the relationship between a company and vendors. But significant combination is not available on customer-product situation.

Customer life cycle management is nothing but input for CRM. The life cycle of customer basically follows the following stages:

(a) Customer acquisition
(b) Personalization and customization
(c) Cross-selling, up-selling and referrals
(d) Customer migration

Customer acquisition is possible via different marketing avenues like traditional mass media advertisement. The objective is to generate more customers and retain them in the future.

The information technology revolution and, in particular, the World Wide Web (WWW) has made available opportunities to companies to decide how they want to interact with their customers. The information technology allows companies to respond directly to customer request and to provide customer with highly interactive, customized experiences. The web-based services have provided a greater opportunity today to establish, nurture and sustain long-term customer relationships than ever before. These online capabilities have increased personal interactions provided through sales people, customer service representatives and call centres. Companies can choose to exploit the low cost web customer service to reduce their service cost. The interaction via web offers the flexibility to select people to whom they wish to offer services and at what quality level.

The internet and other virtual communication portals open the world of global competition to even the smallest companies, levelling the playing field and boosting the customer expectations. The CRM involves far more than just automating processes, marketing, services and then increasing the efficiency of these processes. It involves conducting interactions with customers on a more informed basis and individually tailoring them to customer's needs. A company's CRM solution must support all channels of customer interactions—phone, fax, e-mail, web, wireless devices or face-to-face contact. It must also connect seamlessly with all front and back office enterprise applications and all other business functions as well with the external suppliers and business partners.

Apart from making markets more transparent and available anytime, anywhere, the internet has also brought some fundamental changes within the organization. It helps collaboration in the area of engineering, logistics, vendor management and other value added services. The increasing importance of computing devices will rapidly extend the same capabilities to the field and mobile users as well.

Customer Relationship Management may convey a standard meaning to all categories of people but a problem in CRM means different things to different people. To some, CRM means mailing to customers or mass customization or developing products that fit individual customer's needs. To information technology consultants, CRM is translated into complicated technical jargons related to terms such as Online Analytical Processing (OLAP) and Customer Interaction Centres (CICs).

As a first necessary step, the issue should be clearly supported by top-level. The focus of the organization should be on customer orientation. As a result, a necessary task is the construction of the customer database or information file. This is the foundation of any CRM activity. Companies have traditionally used a variety of methods to construct databases. In manufacturing, it is difficult to develop the customer databases. Normally 20% to 30% response rates are available, leaving big gaps in the database. Service industry is normally in better shape since it involves the kind of customer-company interaction that naturally leads to better data collection.

SPOTLIGHT

Banks have been in the forefront of CRM for a number of years. In India, banks are offering credit card services and they maintain a very good database. Companies offering mobile phone services also maintain strong customer databases. The cost of database is very high to a bank. They can convert a savings bank account holder to a credit card holder with the help of existing data. The analysis helps them to evaluate the potential of the customer to be a credit card holder.

For web-based business, constructing a database should be relatively a straightforward task, as the customer transaction and contact information are accumulated as a natural part of the interaction with customers. But to the brick-and-mortar companies that have not previously collected much customer information, the task is difficult and will involve seeking historical customer contact data from internal sources like accounting and customer service.

Customer Relationship Management requires a substantial amount of investment not only in technology but also in human factors. It is also required to carry out a cost-benefit analysis of CRM investments. Marketing managers of frequently purchased products like soap are not likely to find CRM investments paying out to the extent that would happen in respect of computer servers. The difficulties of reaching customers and attaining the profit margin of the respective products are quite different. Even soap manufacturing companies are using web to differentiate their brands from the myriad of other products appearing in the super markets. This is the evidence that there are perhaps a few companies that cannot benefit from the CRM structure.

12.2 CUSTOMER RELATIONSHIP MANAGEMENT (CRM)

Customer Relationship Management (CRM) is certainly a sound concept that has gained a lot of ground. The hype was high and oversold to the point where many people in the industry tended to see the tools and the technology as ends in themselves, and underestimated the complexity of process and organizational change. The hype is an extremely helpful and factual observation of how new technologies and concepts move from the pioneer phase through a reality check to the mainstream. Numerous studies and surveys from many reputable companies (Forrester, Gartner, Hewson, IDC, Meta) show the limited success rates of CRM projects. There were many problems in CRM project implementation. Some of the most common problems are listed below.

(a) Unrealistically wide project scope
(b) Lack of clear business case and objectives
(c) An IT-led project
(d) Thinking of CRM as a system
(e) Inefficient changes in management resources
(f) Complex international projects with little business justification
(g) Poor project management

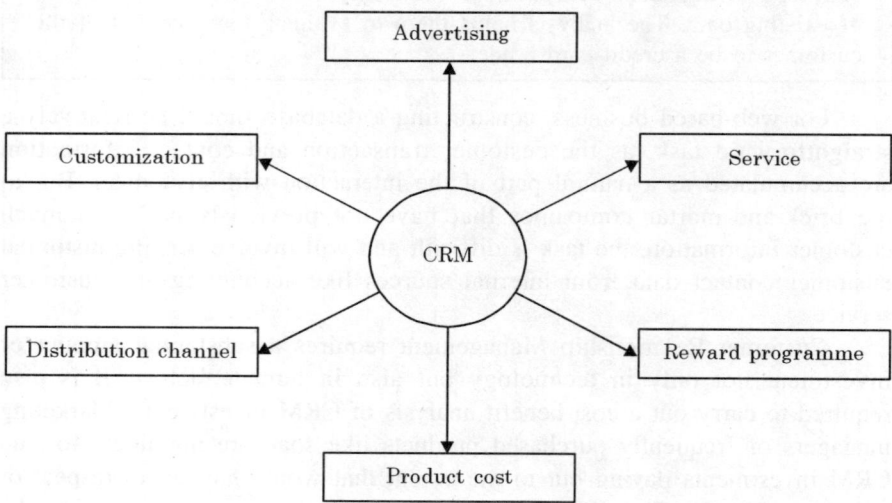

Figure 12.1 Customer Relationship Management (CRM) at work.

On the other hand, CRM revenue grew at a feverish 71% growth rate and reached $ 3.3 billion in 1999. IDC's annual series of forecasts and analysis reports provide five-year forecast for specific software markets. The report estimates of total revenue by customer relationship application packages is not specific to any industry. The sales automation market grew by 54% to $ 1.3 billion, marketing automation by 91% to $ 0.6 billion, customer support and call centre application by 82% to $ 1.3 billion. Research firms had forecast that the revenue growth in the CRM sector would become a $ 12.1 billion market by 2004.

The **benefits** of CRM are manifold. It has serveral **advantages** over traditional mass media marketing. The benefits are as follows:

(a) Reduces advertising cost
(b) Makes it easy to target specific customers by focusing on their needs
(c) Allows companies to compete for customers based on service, not prices.
(d) Prevents overspending on low-value clients or underspending on high-value ones.
(e) Improves the use of the customer channel, thus making the most of each contact with a customer.

In the preceding part, we discussed several issues relating to failures from the beginning to maturity phases. Customer Relationship Management has been showing results in different sectors of business. It begins with the development of a marketing strategy based on the critical forces that effect organizations, such as regulatory, societal, market, technological and business coordinations. Thus marketing strategy is a foundation; the organizations begin to define segments within its current and prospective customer base. The next step is to develop a campaign targeted at one or more of these segments. If the campaign is predicted to be profitable, the content—the message—of the campaign is created; while the content is being created, the organization usually begins scoring its customer database to find potential candidates for the campaign. The customer database contains a list of existing customers, customers who have recently defected, prospective customers, and customers who have affinity to competitors or a combination of all of these. The customers in this database have already been categorized in the earlier segmentation stages. Scoring is a process of using the segments and other customer information to select the customers who are most likely to accept the offer.

There are a number of software products available to assist the CRM process. The database management software allows managing the whole process and analysing for future prediction. Customer Relationship Management allows a company to address all types of customers. It focuses on different points in their life cycle and helps to choose the marketing programme that best fits a customer's attitude towards the company. It can also justify the willingness on the part of the customer to purchase a company's products and services.

12.3 CUSTOMER VALUE MANAGEMENT

Products have their own values to a customer. "Value for money" is a commonly used expression in an organization. Customers treat a product from different angles such as application, usage, price, features, etc. The biggest problem today is how to continue to attract customers and attain growth where products and prices among competitors are more or less the same. Traditional bases such as price, features, etc. are becoming less tangible. So, companies are now using the customer value management approach. The "value" is not only by products but also by process and services. The "ideal customer defined value" is the important aspect to the organization today.

Product value is a dynamic concept. A computer and the chip used inside have different values to a customer. Value proposition should be clear, concise, credible and consistent over time. The value mainly consists of three components as follows:

- Quality
- Services
- Price

Extracting key differentiators from one or more of these core elements provides the basis of an organization's value proposition. A second set of variables comprises image, innovation and intangibles. A good value proposition is difficult to imitate. Because all organizations are separate entities, ideally they should each have their own identities. This requires a careful analysis of all potential value proposition ingredients. The more unique the articulation of the core and augmented value proposition elements are the more memorable will be the message and more likely the success.

There are many online book stores, but amazon.com has captured a huge customer base by offering affordable, easy-to-use services with graphics, excellent contents like information, entertainment and communication features. It has a solid infrastructure and good advertising support. A value proposition is more than just a cute slogan; it is a corporate commitment to pursue a specific strategic direction. An expanded value proposition from a health care provider is possible to be calculated in quantitative terms.

Value proposition = Benefit − Cost
Value proposition = (Quality + Service + Intangibles) − (Price + Non-monetary costs)

The value equation clarifies how consumers measure value in this context.

Transforming a company using CRM requires a balanced and disciplined approach in order to align, link and manage all critical business elements. The focus of the management is to be truly inclined to customer value management. It requires a top-down approach throughout the organization based on the factors listed below:

- Business Direction
    (a) Target market and segment
    (b) Customer needs
    (c) Deliverables—product, marketing and relationship
- Core Competencies
    (a) Technical competencies
    (b) Business process capabilities
    (c) Brand
    (d) Regional/country-specific
- Infrastructure
    (a) Organizational structure
    (b) Human resources
    (c) Culture
    (d) Assets and final resources
    (e) Information Technology (IT)

Customer value management based transformation requires the development of a customer-defined vision of ideal outcomes from doing business with the company. The company must have a clear definition of who the target customers are. Segmentation of market place on at least two dimensions—current and potential profitability—is an important factor to start with. Without these, a vision, though clearly defined and communicated to the full management team, to become the premiere service/product to customers is not focused and workable.

Now let us consider the customer value management approach or process based on which the required deliverables are to be achieved. Once the segmentation has been targeted and actionable needs/wants/values determined, the company must define the critical things at which it must be competent.

The competencies identified might include the capabilities to:

- Understand customers' requests.
- Make a valid commitment, including the commitment of all relevant cross-functional resources.
- Communicate to all involved in the value chain.
- Identify critical path and take action to generate on-time delivery.
- Ensure quality workmanship.
- Provide contact point in each medium the customer wishes to use.

- Ensure that the contact staff can deliver cross-functional information, commit action and ensure resolution.

In all cases of company's functions, process and information systems must be evaluated for their ability to undertake the changes required, wherever gaps are revealed.

Infrastructure is a critical success factor in customer value management process. The defined capabilities can be converted to action, only if the infrastructure supports them. The enabling infrastructure might be:

- A single source of database on customers, commitments and relevant aspects of each deal, i.e., products, configurations, services, processes, available inventory, production, delivery schedule, terms and conditions, etc.
- Availability of data at appropriate time and places to all involved in making and delivering the commitment.
- Empowered, qualified, trained and briefed front office and back-office employees who are motivated to meet customer's needs.
- A database of common product faults and remedies.
- Process management discipline.

Next, we are interested in the sources of customer value management information. The source is another contact point to develop customer value engineering process. Traditional sources are market research data, secondary data from agency and government reports, etc. but the following sources are the prime areas considered.

Market segmentation: The transaction data of the company together with the customer data, is mined for clustering of customers. These can be probed to identify common underlying "values" which account for similar behaviour.

Benchmarks of performance: The company looks on the industry and across parallel industry. Customers' needs and perceptions are driven by their experiences, cross-industry and cross-geography, and are not necessarily limited to the customer or to comparisons with direct competitors.

Brainstorming and invention: Major breakthroughs occur as the different functions, processes or companies in the value chain begin to understand their collective relationships and impacts upon the deliverables. Brainstorming sessions help identify the benefits of each function under customer value management.

In the changing customer needs, wants and perceptions of "value" are accelerated by the application of e-business techniques to the relationship between members of the value chain. We have discussed in this chapter the main components of customer value management. The involvement of an external partner may be required in order to attain the benefits from customer value management. As we proceed, many factors are important for the successful implementation of the value management techniques. The following are some of the critical factors for the successful implementation of value management techniques:

- A methodical framework to compete on customer-defined value and to institutionalize customer knowledge.
- Experience in strategy implementation, not just in strategy development.
- Industry knowledge.
- Experience in business process design, development and implementation.
- Understanding of how information technology is deployed at the customer interface and throughout the value chain, in order to maximize customer value and experience in deploying it.

12.4 CUSTOMER RELATIONSHIP MANAGEMENT AND DATA MANAGEMENT

Data management is the basic job in an information system (Figure 12.2). Today, it is possible to maintain a large kind of database with the help of IT. At the same time, software is available to analyse those data. The key characteristic of commercial data is its volume. Millions of individuals in thousands of separate locations can perform hundreds of transactions each, in a short span of time, resulting in billions of countable events. Let us consider the data generated through credit card purchase. It generates hundreds of millions of data items each week. Tracking and understanding this behaviour

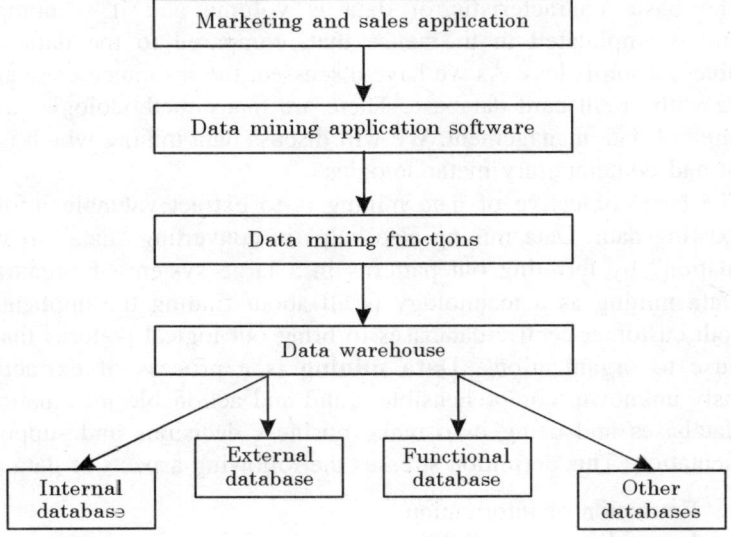

Figure 12.2 Customer Relationship Management and data mining.

involves building a complex and sophisticated system. Examples are endless from business-to-business markets. The important part is to manage customers, products, outlets and the like that aided by a more complete understanding of the current and past activities of a customer. It is useful to formulate initiatives beforehand. Once the process starts, it is not possible to develop the system and data for analysis. But the system should allow means to solve the problem. Three key points arise as follows:

(a) There would be clear-cut and important business problems to be solved.
(b) There is an information-rich environment.
(c) The means to modify the situation exist.

SPOTLIGHT

Insurance companies are under tremendous competition in India. One of the basic premises is that there is huge potential in Indian market. They are developing new products that suit Indian consumers. The premium, one of the factors of decision-making, requires analysis and research before launching their service or product. They cannot share data with existing insurance companies, as because the things are not organized and at the same time, system does not support quick access of information. On the other hand, banks and credit card companies have potential data, which can be used as input for insurance companies. They have developed the system in such a way, which offers flexibility to use the data and extract useful part of it for analysis. So, they are more concerned with developing the existing database rather than something for future projection.

The basic characteristic of data is volume and it is complicated in nature. Complicated in the sense that, compared to the data volume, actionable portion is less. As we have discussed, the insurance companies are working with credit card database. There are many methodologies available in the area of data management. We will discuss data mining which is one of the best and contemporary methodologies.

The basic objective of data mining is to extract valuable information from existing data. Data mining also helps in converting "data" to valuable "information" by ferreting out patterns in a large system of organizational data. Data mining as a technology is all about finding the applications of mammoth customer-centric databases to bring out logical patterns that might be of use to organizations. **Data mining** is a process of extracting the previously unknown, comprehensible, valid and actionable information from large databases and using it to make business decisions and support their implementation. This definition stresses the following aspects of data mining:

- Extraction of information
- Large data responsibilities
- Formulating initiatives

The aim of data mining is to obtain a sufficient understanding of a behavioural pattern of a market to allow quantifiable benefits to be derived from changes in behaviour suggested by the analysis. This involves: learning the previously unknown facts about market, customer, and even forecasting questions.

Data mining is not a miracle science. For the decision to use data mining, organizations must develop a clear view of how they are going to use the results, in policy terms. Companies with large database and strong marketing staff should have moderate knowledge about their customers. Data mining will confirm their beliefs, but add a more quantitative or practical edge. So, data mining starts with the idea that companies hold a lot of data about their business but may not be in a position to fully understand all the details. By "digging" in the data, it is possible to "mine" the nuggets of buried information. But it is more than simple data analysis. It is the understanding of the whole business environment to answer relevant questions with the help of data analysis tool. In another way, it is a machine-aided consultancy. Myths about data mining are common like other Information Technology areas. One is that it is trivial, because it is just running a few off-the-shelf tools. Another myth is that, mining will unlock everything a company needs to know. Myths like these often arise because many suppliers of analytical software call their products data mining software.

In order to build good models for your customer relationship system, there are a number of steps to follow. The cross data mining process model described here is similar to other processes available. One should keep in mind that while the steps appear in a list, the data mining process is not linear. One should look back to the previous steps.

The basic steps of data mining for effective CRM are as follows:

(1) Define business problems
(2) Build marketing database
(3) Explore data
(4) Prepare data for modelling
(5) Build model
(6) Evaluate model
(7) Deploy model and results

Each CRM application has one or more objectives for the business model. The first step, develop the business model, depending on the goal of the organization, such as "increasing the response rate" or "value of response count", etc. The model also includes a way to measure the result of the CRM project.

Steps 2–4 constitute the core of the data preparation. These data preparation steps may take anywhere between 50% and 90% time and effort for the entire data mining process. Marketing database needs to be built, as corporate databases often do not contain the data that one needs for it. They may reside in multiple databases such as, customer database, product database and transaction database. This means integrating and consolidating the data into a single marketing database and reconciling the differences in data values from the various sources. Improper data is a major source of problems.

The third step required is that one should understand data before developing predictive models. Graphic and visualization tools are vital in data presentation. One needs to gather a variety of numerical summaries and define distribution of data.

Preparation of the final data modelling is the last step before building models. It consists of four stages:

(a) Selection of variables on which the model is to be built
(b) Construction of new predictors derived from the raw data
(c) Selection of a subset or sample of data on which model is to be built
(d) Transformation of variables in accordance with the requirements of the algorithm

The most important part to remember about model building is that it is an interactive process. One needs to explore alternative models to find the one that is most useful in solving the business problems. Most CRM applications are based on a protocol called supervised learning. It is recommended to start with customer information for which the desired outcome is already known.

The most overrated metric for evaluating the results is perhaps the accuracy. The last step is incorporation of data mining in the CRM model. In building a CRM application, data mining is often a small, albeit critical part of the final product. Predictive patterns through data mining may be combined with the knowledge of domain experts and incorporated in a large application used by many people.

Database management with the help of data mining has been gaining immense importance in the industry at large. Some popular types of data mining activities encountered in practice are listed below:

- Customer gain and loss analysis
- Customer migration
- Customer solicitation
- Customer response analysis
- Promotion analysis
- Purchase analysis
- Seasonality analysis

In a comparative market, particularly under the changing market conditions, profitability is often closely related to the speed of solving multiple problems. It is recommended that before embarking on a data mining project, one should assess precisely as to how the outcomes are related to marketing strategy.

REVIEW QUESTIONS

1. What do you understand by Customer Relationship Management?
2. What is relationship marketing?
3. List the life cycle of a customer in the light of Customer Relationship Management.
4. What are the common problems in Customer Relationship Management projects?
5. What are the benefits of Customer Relationship Management?
6. List the three sectors where Customer Relationship Management can be implemented.
7. What is customer value management?
8. What do you understand by data mining?
9. List the different steps in data mining for effective Customer Relationship Management.
10. What is data modelling in Customer Relationship Management?

DISCUSSION QUESTIONS

1. Product value is a dynamic concept. Discuss this statement in the light of Customer Relationship Management.
2. What are the various sources of customer value management?
3. Data mining is to extract valuable information from existing data. Explain this statement in the light of Customer Relationship Management.

13
Decision Support System

13.1 INTRODUCTION

Information plays a major role in any organization. The value of information depends on its application and use. The success of an organization largely depends on the quality of the information that it generates. The information is used as raw material for decision-making. Computer Based Information Systems (CBIS) can make the process effective and efficient when large amounts of data are involved. There are several types of information systems that support decision-making. The Decision Support System (DSS) is one of them.

Academic researchers have built and investigated DSS for more than 35 years. DSS started in the era of distributed computing. The idea evolved in the area of applied information technology. It involves people, system and information technology. Prior to 1965, it was expensive to build and manage large-scale information systems. But after the development of the IBM system 360 and more powerful mainframe systems, it became more practical and cost effective to develop management information systems. In the late 1960s, a new type of information system was developed—a model based on DSS or management decision systems. In the late 1970s, both practical and theoretical issues related to DSS were discussed in various seminar and conferences. A number of companies had developed information systems that used data and models to help managers analyse semi-structured problems. This system was named Decision Support System. It was recognized from that time that DSS could be designed to support decision-makers at any level in an organization. It could support financial management, operations and strategic decision-making.

In the mid-1980s, academic researchers developed a new kind of software to support group decision-making. Many research studies have examined the impact and consequences of the Group Decision Support System (GDSS). Also a number of organizations have commercialized the group decision support system and groupware product.

In the field of Executive Information System (EIS) evolved from single-user, model-driven DSS and improved rational database products, the first EIS was maintained by analysts for senior executives. Beginning in 1990, data warehousing and OLAP began broadening the area of executive information system. Another broader category was developed, namely the data-driven decision support system.

In the early 1990s, a shift occurred from mainframe-based decision support system to the client-server-based decision support system. Some products on desktop Online Analytical Processing (OLAP) tools were introduced during this time period. In 1992–93, some vendors recommended object-oriented technology for decision support capabilities. In the same period, data warehouse was completed, which is an object-oriented technology. In 1994, large companies started to upgrade their network infrastructure. In 1995, World Wide Web (WWW) began to impact academics and practitioners in decision support technologies. Web-based and web-enabled decision support system had become feasible in about 1995.

The concepts and technologies of DSS are still evolving. Today the internet and web-based technologies like mobile commerce have opened up developments in DSS and have made it hard to keep up with the rapid changes in DSS capabilities.

DSS covers a wide variety of systems, tools and technologies. Some people think that the term Decision Support System is outdated and it has been replaced by a new type of system called Online Analytical Processing (OLAP). Other views emphasize creating knowledge-based decision support systems as state-of-the-art in DSS. Operation researchers primarily focus on optimization and simulation models as the real DSS. Academics have different meaning and connotation as discussed in research areas of DSS. Actually, the term Decision Support System and its acronym DSS is useful and an inclusive term for many types of information systems that support decision-making. A Decision Support System is not only confined to computer-based or OLAP system, but it is equally important for manual data processing. Today, a numbers of tools are available in the market and companies have adopted customized products on Decision Support System (DSS). If a software program runs on a PC and can help a manager to make decisions, then someone will most likely refer to it as DSS. Executive Information System (EIS), Executive Support System (ESS), Geographic Information System (GIS), OnLine Analytical Processing (OLAP), software agents, knowledge discovery or management systems and Group Decision Support System (GDSS), can all be implemented into the category named DSS.

So, how do information system managers and business executives discuss constructing the Decision Support System (DSS) that the executives really want? How do we sort out all the noisy surroundings, this catch-all term decision support systems? The answer lies in gaining as much knowledge as you can about DSS. It requires a common understanding for both the future executives and the information system managers. Knowledge business executives should speak candidly with the information system staff about deliverables, capabilities, outcomes, needs and what decisions should be supported by a proposed system. The two major categories involved are the enterprise-wise decision support system and the desktop decision support system.

An enterprise-wise decision support system is linked to a large, data warehouse and serves many managers in a company. A desktop, single-user decision support system consists of small systems that reside in an individual executive's PC. These two types include a broad range of functional areas. Much excitement surrounds the development of enterprise-wise decision support systems, with a very large data warehouse that supposedly help decision-makers to find out almost anything about their organization in a matter of time. Decision makers can slice and dice, graph and chart corporate data as well as external data.

In this chapter, we will discuss the following tools used in DSS.

- Communication driven decision support system
- Data driven decision support system
- Document driven decision support system
- Model driven decision support system

Each of the tools will be discussed with some software products available under this category.

Decision Support Systems are computer-based information systems designed in such a way that help managers select one of the many alternative solutions to a problem. It is possible to automate some of the decision-making processes in a large, computer-based DSS which is sophisticated and analyse vast amount of information fast. It helps corporates to increase market share, reduce costs, increase profitability and enhance quality. Software increases the efficiency of a system when all other components of the system are synergized. The problem itself plays the main role in a process of decision-making.

The problem can be classified as structured, semi-structured and unstructured, i.e. the problem can vary from structured to unstructured or may fall between two extremes as semi-structured. A structured problem is one where the optimum solution can be reached through known steps. The sequence of steps is technically known as algorithm. The same data will always yield the same solution when it passes through the algorithm.

An unstructured problem is one when it is not possible to reach an optimal solution. In this case, enough information may not be available or there may exist many potential factors that no algorithm can be formulated to work out a unique optimal solution. An unstructured problem is closely related to the uncertain nature of the problem.

A semi-structured problem is one that is neither structured nor totally unstructured. It may be possible to work out the optimal solution based on the criticality of the problem. It requires expertise in that field to find out the number of different possible solutions.

SPOTLIGHT

In a toy manufacturing company, the sales department sends monthly sales information to the marketing department. Based on the information on market research data and sales figure of last three years, the marketing department forecasts sales data for one calendar year. Sales data for each month are given to the production department. The production department produces the product based on forecast. In each quarter, actual sales figures are collected and compared with the forecasted data. The method is followed throughout the year. Two departments are involved here. In the beginning, decision is made based on forecasted figure. But the actual figures may vary significantly, since there are other factors that had not been possible to be estimated. As the number of factors which influence the forecast increases, the decision-making process gets more complicated. A computer-based decision support system works efficiently under this situation. In this case, the problem is semi-structured. As the number factors gradually increases, the problem gets unstructured and it is not possible to manage manually.

13.2 COMMUNICATION DRIVEN DECISION SUPPORT SYSTEM

It emphasizes communication, collaboration and shared decision-making support. A communication driven decision support system enables communication between groups of people, facilitates sharing of information, supports collaboration and coordination between people, and supports group decision tasks. A simple bulletin board or threaded e-mail is the most basic level of functionality. Here, a group of people work together using various software tools. Video conferencing, bulletin board, audio conferencing, electronic mail, document sharing, and interactive videos are examples of group support tools. Vendors, consultants, users and researchers all refer to them as groupware. It enables the group members to generate, read and organize information in a structured manner. The internet infrastructure is an important factor enabling the development of more powerful groupware systems. Newsgroup is very good at enabling many people to generate information, but who lack the ability to organize the information. Newsgroup enables the group to edit, store, delete and structure information that is easy to analyse and can evolve progressively as new information is added. This form of groupware is used in special purpose meeting rooms, as well as to enable groups to 'meet' from different geographic locations.

The virtual workplace is another area of collaborative computing environment, designed to support temporarily and geographically dispersed work teams. It is a framework for integrating the diverse collaborative capabilities.

Many software products are available to support communication driven decision support systems. Web-based software is designed to support the work of virtual teams working on complex projects.

Communication driven decision support systems have generated a lot of interest in research people. Key research areas include impact of group processes and group awareness, multi-user interfaces, concurrency control, communication and co-ordination within the group. A communication driven decision support system is often categorized according to the time or location matrix using the distinction between the same time and same place (face to face) or different time and different place (distributed).

13.3 DATA DRIVEN DECISION SUPPORT SYSTEM

A data driven decision support system is a type of decision support system that emphasizes access to and manipulation of internal and external data. A database or data warehouse allows a decision-maker to capture data and prepare reports. Data is the prime material, which allows the user to generate information. Simple file systems accessed by query and retrieval tools provide the most elementary level. A data warehouse system that allows the manipulation of data by computerized tools tailored to a specific task and setting or by more general tools and operators, provides additional functionality.

A data driven decision support system with OLAP provides the highest level of functionality and decision support that is linked to analyse large collections of historical data. The Executive Information System (EIS) and the Geographic Information System (GIS) are the special purpose data driven decision support systems. A data management module accesses the data and provides a means for the DSS to select data based on different criteria: a data driven decision support system is more concerned with historical data rather than transactional data. A data driven decision support system may use a database created for the system, but usually it is linked to other databases.

Data warehouse is a subject-oriented, integrated, time variant, non-volatile collection of data to support management decision-making processes. A data warehouse contains a large amount of data. It is batch updated and structured for rapid online queries for managerial decision-making. OLAP software is used for manipulating data from a variety of sources that have been stored in a data warehouse. An OLAP software product must contain three key features:

- Multidimensional views of data
- Time-oriented processing capabilities
- Complex calculations

The software creates various views and representations.

OLAP was introduced first by E.F. Codd, the father of relational database. New acronyms have flourished, which go from ROLAP to MOLAP via DOLAP. Originally, OLAP defined the rules to characterize technology. Basically it follows the multidimensional model, transparency of the server, client server architecture, multi-user, flexible posting and editing of data, multiple dimensions and levels, management of data scarcity, etc. OLAP can be used in large databases. Two of the favourite areas are sales analysis and marketing. They help to study the volume of sales by product, region and time. One can forecast the changes in the sales data in a year. It has many applications in internet-based databases.

Executive Information Systems are computerized systems intended to provide current and appropriate information to the executives using a networked workstation. The emphasis is on geographical displays and an easy-to-use interface that presents information from the corporate database. EISs offer strong reporting and drill-down capabilities. A GIS or Spatial Decision Support System is a support system that uses maps to represent information. It helps people access, display and analyse data that have geographic content and meaning.

SPOTLIGHT

An equity analyst always needs access to current stock price and those from at least the few preceding years. The analyst plays an advisory role in their relationship with the client. He keeps data on economic, business details and price movement for three to four years. He can forecast the future trend of the price movement based on that stored information. Software packages retrieve data from data stores. It is nothing but a data management module which access the data and provides a mean for the Decision Support System (DSS) to select the data based on different criteria: types of stock, years under study, past trend and so on. Business houses are enjoying those benefits to improve their productivity.

13.4 DOCUMENT DRIVEN DECISION SUPPORT SYSTEM

A document driven decision support system is a relatively new field in decision support. This system is basically focused on retrieval and management of unstructured documents. Documents can be presented in three categories:

(a) Oral
(b) Written
(c) Video

Examples of oral documents are the conversations that are transcribed; television commercials, news clips are examples of video. Written documents comprise reports, catalogues, letters from customers, memos, e-mails, etc.

In an organization, executives store documents which eat up huge floor space, cabinets, etc. It is interesting to note that out of all those documents, only ten to fifteen percent are available to executives for the use of decision-making. Documents are not standardized in a uniform pattern or structure. But by nature, people are not inclined to structure the system. The job of senior executives and information technology people is to correlate their documents into usable formats that can be compared and processed. They also incorporate databases to support decision-making.

Document driven decision support systems have been gaining importance because of the development of internet. New technology and software is turning this concept into a reality. Basic document driven systems exist in the form of web-based search engines, like google, excite, alta vista and lycos. Search engines allow users to input words or phrases in order to specify and obtain the documents of their choice.

Many software packages are available, which allow the user to search a specific document in a special manner. The software first searches through different search engines and results are stored with the search site. It helps user locate all search results at one go, collected from different search engines. Further advances in client/server technology will allow executives to store, manage and access these documents.

E-mail is one of the widely used communication media all over the world. While academics are putting emphasis on the way in which e-mails can be abused by the employees, there has been much less attention paid to the issues of the time that employees now spend managing the e-mail traffic. This problem can arise when e-mails are not integrated with the other company information, such as project or case files. Today, software packages reduce the work load associated with managing e-mails and improve retrieval time by automatically indexing e-mails and filing them in such a way that they can be easily found by users searching a project, case or customer file. Another major benefit is the ability to control e-mails as corporate records—an increasingly necessary requirement by companies for regulatory purposes.

Document converter is another product under this category. It enables to convert large number of documents at one time, instead of trying to do them individually.

13.5 MODEL DRIVEN DECISION SUPPORT SYSTEM

The model driven decision support system emphasizes access to and manipulation of a model that is financial, statistical, optimization and/or simulation. Simple analytical and statistical tools provide the most elementary level. In general, the model driven decision support system uses complex financial simulation, and optimization or multi-criteria model to help decision support. A sequence of events, or a pattern of behaviour, may become a useful model, when the relationship among inputs, outputs and conditions can be established well enough that they can be used to analyse different parameters. Models are based on mathematical research or on experience.

The OLAP system allows complex and difficult analysis of data. The model driven decision support system uses data and parameters provided by decision makers to aid them in interpreting and analysing a situation.

There are many models available to analyse the input data for decision-making process. Decision analysis tools help decision-makers to decompose and structure problems. The aim of these tools is to help a user in the application of models like trees, multi-attributed utility models, etc.

The forecasting support system is a computer-based system that supports users in making and evaluating forecasts. The user can analyse time series data. Many statistical tools are available under this category. Among the general type of statistical models, linear regression model is the best-fitted linear relationship between two variables. Linear programming is a mathematical model for the optimal solution of resource allocation problems. Simulation is a technique for conducting one or more experiments that test various outcomes resulting from a quantitative model of a system.

Decision Support System (DSS) can be augmented using decision tree analysis. Figure 13.1 shows a decision tree for developing a software product. The organization can choose among one of the following decisions:

(a) Build the software
(b) Reuse the existing software with modifications
(c) Buy the product with modification
(d) Contract the product to an outside vendor

A decision tree consists of branches and subbranches. Decisions are denoted through branches with probability. At the end of the tree, different costs are available. The total probability through any branch should be one. In the given example, in case of reuse, the probability of no change is 0.40 and cost is Rs. 275,000. On the other hand, in the case of change the probability is 0.60 with two subbranches. In the first subbranch, simple case, the probability is 0.20 and the cost is Rs. 410,000. In the case of complex case, the probability is 0.80 and the cost is Rs. 500,000. In the main branch, the probability for change and no change is 0.40 + 0.60 = 1. In the sub-branch of change, the probability of simple and complex is 0.20 + 0.80 = 1.

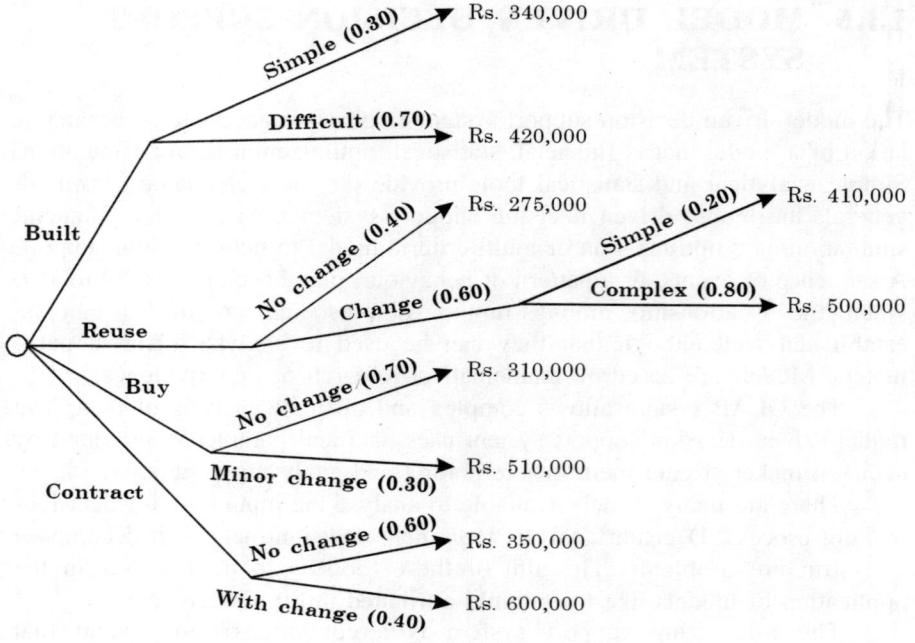

Figure 13.1 Decision tree.

If the product is built, there is 70% probability that the job will be difficult. The project cost in that case is Rs. 420,000. On the other hand, that is, in the simple case, the cost is Rs. 340,000.

The expected cost can be computed along any branch of the decision tree.

Expected cost = Σ (Path probability) × (Estimated cost of the path)

For the built path,

Expected cost = 0.30 × Rs. 340,000 + 0.70 × Rs. 420,000
= Rs. 396,000

Expected cost for reuse = 0.40 × Rs. 275,000 + 0.60
(0.20 × Rs. 410,000 + 0.80 × Rs. 500,000)
= Rs. 110,000 + Rs. 289,200
= Rs. 399,200

Expected cost for buy = 0.70 × Rs. 300,000 + 0.30 × Rs. 510,000
= Rs. 370,000

Expected cost for contract = 0.60 × Rs. 350,000 + 0.40 × Rs. 600,000
= Rs. 390,000

Based on the estimated cost as discussed before, the lowest expected cost is the buy option. So it is recommended to buy the product. But the cost is not the only option for decision-making. One must consider the other factors in decision-making process as well. It is possible to develop matrices for other factors in decision-making process.

Simulation is a method for decision-making by designing, constructing and manipulating a model of the real system. It is a useful technique for solving business problems where many values of the variables are not known or partly known. Simulation technique is useful in analysing a complex system, where the analytical method is either difficult or not known. Simulation method is useful in the following cases:

(a) Man-hiring decisions
(b) Transport scheduling
(c) Evaluating an alternative investment analysis
(d) Traffic light timing

A trader deals in a perishable commodity. The trader buys the commodity at Rs. 20/kg and sells at Rs. 30/kg. Excess stock has no saleable value and cost is Rs. 8/kg. He likes to develop a purchase pattern, where the loss will be minimum. It is possible to simulate the data through a computer program. The purchase data and the market demand is required to be input to the computer. It is possible to develop this model by the spread-sheet program.

Demand	No. of days	Sold	No. of days
1	40	1	50
2	50	2	110
3	200	3	210
4	160	4	100
5	90	5	70
	540		540

Demand	Probability		Sold	Probability	
1	0.07	0 – 6	1	0.09	0 – 8
2	0.09	7 – 15	2	0.20	9 – 28
3	0.37	16 – 52	2	0.39	29 – 67
4	0.30	53 – 82	2	0.19	68 – 86
5	0.17	83 – 100	2	0.13	87 – 100
	1.00			1.00	

(a)	(b)	(c)	(d)	(e)	(f)	(g)	(h)			
Day	Random No.	Purchase	Random No.	Demand	Purchase cost	Selling price	Excess stock	Cost	Profit	Profit/ Loss
1	29	3	28	2	60	60	1	8	0	−8
2	68	4	65	3	80	90	1	8	10	2
3	18	3	90	5	60	150	–		90	90
4	81	4	27	2	80	60	2	16		−16
5	78	4	59	3	80	90	1	8	10	2
6	12	2	46	3	40	90	–		50	50
7	69	4	5	1	80	30	3	24		−24
8	39	3	91	5	60	150	–		90	90
9	39	3	60	3	60	90	–		30	30
10	60	4	69	4	80	80	–		0	0
										216

From the simulation, the trader makes a net profit of Rs. 216. But the number of simulations is too small to draw inference.

It is possible to simulate a large number of times with the help of the computer. It is also possible to develop programs, where the number of simulations is in the hands of users.

Not all decision support system are business oriented. Some areas, especially engineering models in DSS, may simulate physical environment rather than business environment.

Models are developed through life cycle phases. It starts with goal identification. The following chart (Figure 13.2) shows the tasks involved in modifying the life cycle.

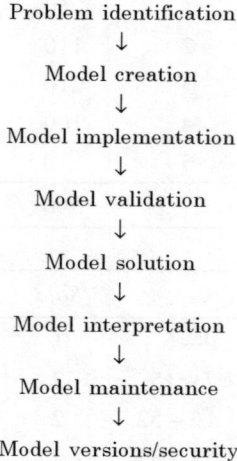

Problem identification
↓
Model creation
↓
Model implementation
↓
Model validation
↓
Model solution
↓
Model interpretation
↓
Model maintenance
↓
Model versions/security

Figure 13.2 Tasks in modifying a life cycle.

Models are developed based on different attributes and tested under long complex situations. The model driven decision support system has been playing a major role in organization. The hardware cost has come down, which helps to implement those models through costly complex software.

13.6 TREND IN DECISION SUPPORT SYSTEM

Vendors now offer off-the-shelf DSS, but many organizations develop their own systems, if the systems have to deal with unique problems of the organization. Globalization has changed the ways of running business as competition is the buzzword today. Companies are busy finding out different measures to cut down costs at various levels. Information technology has changed the way of decision-making. Acquisition of a new DSS needs to be justified in terms of the need of investment in employee time and efforts to develop a new one and understand the compromises involved in using a readymade off-the-shelf product.

There are essentially three layers of technology in an organization:

(1) Transactional systems that include legacy systems, accounting packages and Enterprise Resource Planning (ERP)
(2) Analytical systems that include planning, reporting and consolidation
(3) Decision Support Systems

Most of the organizations have implemented the first layer. The second layer consists of spreadsheet-based solution or best-of-breed solution. Most of the organizations have not implemented the third level. To build a true decision support system, organizations must integrate all three layers with an interface that is easily accessible throughout the organization.

Organizations have data in different system locations. The data in these systems need to be exported, transferred and loaded into a centralized storage area, commonly referred to as a data warehouse where the data is then typically organized into cubes so that it can be viewed three dimensionally. It is nothing but data mining. Here the "slice" of data from the cube may include sales by product or by area. The user can drill-down the data for more details on different cubes.

Business intelligence must be applied to the data to make it relevant to the organization. However, organizations now have measures, or Key Performance Indicator (KPI) for every business unit and departments within the enterprise.

Web-based technology has been emerging throughout the world. Organizations have started delivering service through websites in addition to existing brick-and-mortar business. The virtual office is a reality today. The group decision support system has changed the role of the employee in the organization. In addition, various researches have been taken place in artificial intelligence in business. Robotics engineers build machines to perform useful work. In artificial intelligence, various subfields have been developed for DSS. Those systems are artificial vision, natural language processing, expert systems, neutral networks, fuzzy logic, genetic algorithms and intelligent agents.

In an expert system, the ability of a computer lies in replicating the true human expertise. The objective is to develop a system that could diagnose human diseases, better than a human expert. The process is not easy to be developed and is expensive too. The data, which are knowledge-based, contain rules, facts and descriptions of objects. An expert system cell is a collection of programs for processing. It also has one interface engine, which communicates via user interface.

Expert system technology is an outgrowth of a field of study called **Artificial Intelligence (AI)**. Smart computer programs have been replacing factory workers. Artificial Intelligence is moving from research lab to business, industrial and professional applications. AI technology, however, places much greater emphasis on the specific knowledge which a particular task requires rather than on the computational power it demands. It may be possible for a programmer to write code in simple cases. For example, playing tick-toe is possible to list in every situation and the corresponding move, so that the machine can decide what to do at each step by simply looking at the appropriate move on the list. But for complex tasks, like playing chess, this approach is not feasible. It is very difficult to write down as a conventional program. The decisions are far too complex to be exhaustively described by tables or procedures. Still they seem to be made by the application of a large collection of rules of thumb that are well explained by situation-action rules. The knowledge happens to be captured in a form that allows it to be applied mechanically, so that the task can be completely automated. AI systems are designed to help only one component of a task and the human user is left to interpret the output.

Another important aspect is that most AI systems are highly specialized experts but have no basic capabilities to solve other problems, even the general ones. For example, program experts on infectious diseases know nothing of general medicine. The simpler and more general problems are in fact harder to solve with the existing AI techniques.

Thus limited ability to capture knowledge sharply constrains the kind of AI applications. So, the focus is on rather narrow domains of knowledge.

The fundamental issues for operational deployment are predictability and accountability. Naively constructed AI systems typically have neither. So, the operational issue must be addressed for commercial applications. Solution may be to concentrate on low responsibility applications in which the consequences of errors are nil. Another approach is to package AI technology as an assistant rather than as a primary decision-maker.

Artificial Intelligence refers to a group of related disciplines (Figure 13.3).

Here natural language concerns the development of the human language

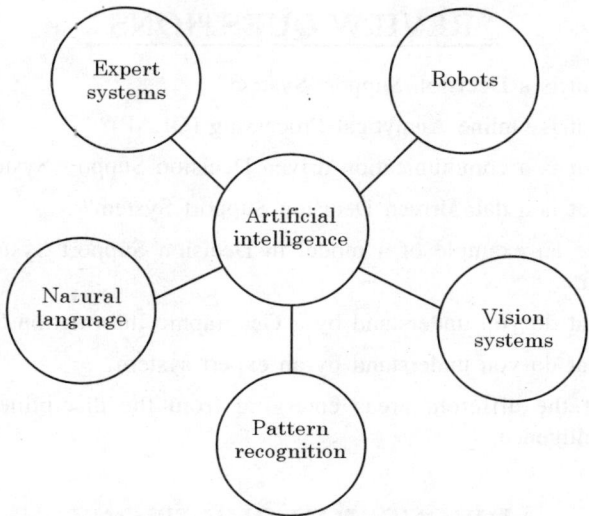

Figure 13.3 Artificial intelligence discipline.

computer interface and translation. The AI software can recognize human voice and can receive dictation. Pattern recognition systems provide the technology to identify patterns like visual, auditory and other signals. Vision system allows the computer system to "see". Banks use this technology to identify customers. Robotics concerns the development of industrial robotics. It is very useful in production, where the environment is uncomfortable.

Most of the large, well-known AI systems use a software technology very different from that employed in general application. The more sophisticated AI development environment provides much greater power where that is appropriate to the problem.

Here the investment is often great, because it involves the time of both highly paid experts and knowledge engineers. Therefore, justification of cost is equally important.

Expert systems offer valuable contributions to business houses. Even the cost of developing some systems is very high in many cases; the benefits can outweigh the expenses. The greatest benefit of an expert system is their contribution to high productivity thereby helping the employees to save their time.

It may still be difficult to establish information requirements even with the use of critical success factors and other methods. Senior manager's decision-making may not be supported by the information system because the decisions are too unstructured and fluid. For instance, top-level executives may not agree on firm's success factors, or the factors they describe may be inappropriate or outdated even when the firm is confronting a crisis which requires a major strategic change.

REVIEW QUESTIONS

1. What is a Decision Support System?
2. What is Online Analytical Processing (OLAP)?
3. What is a communication driven Decision Support System?
4. What is a data driven Decision Support System?
5. Give an example of a model in Decision Support System to process data.
6. What do you understand by a Geographic Information System?
7. What do you understand by an expert system?
8. List the different areas emerging from the discipline of Artificial Intelligence.

DISCUSSION QUESTIONS

1. Decision Support Systems structure an unstructured decision making process. Explain with examples.
2. "Decision Support Systems use models to process information. Explain this statement.
3. Give three examples of a business decision, which you would use in your Decision Support System model.

14

Executive Information System

14.1 INTRODUCTION

The term executive is applied in different connotations. Executives are defined not in terms of personal characteristics but in terms of the job. The work area is an important criteria to justify the position of an executive. On the other hand, hierarchy could help to draw distinction as an executive. In addition to their long-term horizon, executives can often be distinguished from others in the organization at lower levels by their attitude. Management theorists have given their own insights into executives. Henri Fayol believed that all managers perform the same functional job like planning, organizing, staffing, directing and controlling. As per Henry Mintzberg, all managers' roles may be same but orientation is different at each level. John P. Kotter, professor from Harvard believes that executives follow a three-step strategy. First, they establish agenda, secondly build networks and finally establish the right network.

Figure 14.1 shows that the Executive Information System (EIS) sits on top of the functional systems. The triangular figure does not represent the size of the functional area, i.e. the size has nothing to do with the functional area. The size of the manpower in the functional area depends on the type of organization or the business they are in. For example, a company in business of call centres have maximum number of employees at the operation level compared to other functional areas like marketing, support staff, etc. On the other hand, in a manufacturing company, the financial department has less people than those in the production department. The executive information system is formed by a group of selected people from all the functional areas and are involved in decision-making. It is not like a typical functional area like marketing or finance but a combination of all these areas which may not exist as a separate function, like a shop-floor under the production

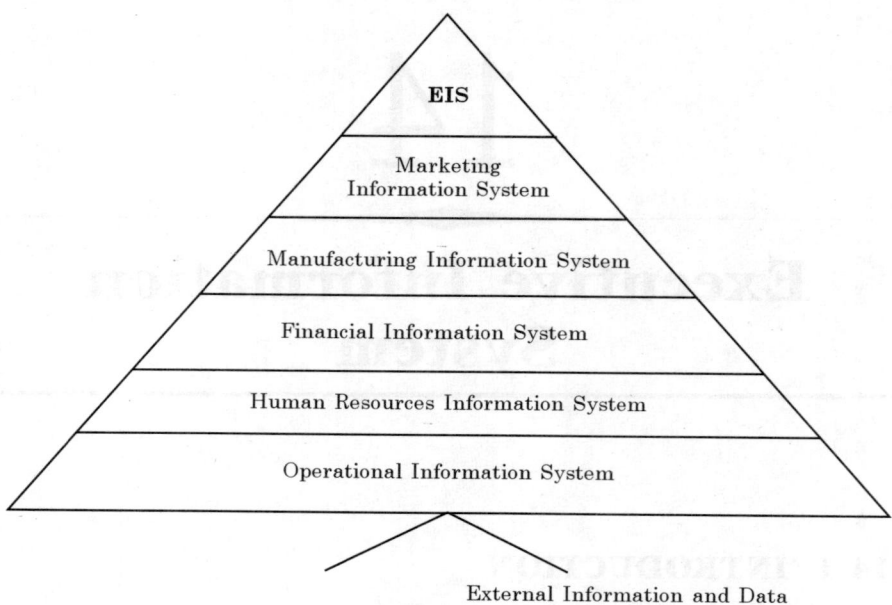

Figure 14.1 Executive Information System (EIS).

department in the organization. In many cases, store and purchase comes under accounts and finance department but in the executive information system, stores and purchase play major roles even though they are not treated as separate departments in the organization. The pieces of information are processed and produced within the firm and the environment. External information is generally important at the top level. At the higher level of the hierarchy, executives obtain information from reports generated by the lower level. The distance separates them from the physical location in many cases.

The early Executive Information System was tailored to the demands of a specific executive, but this approach had many shortcomings. First, executives found that their juniors did not have the same data what they themselves carried. In many cases, the same data were collected from different locations. In addition, briefing books were inflexible—they were essentiality reports on screen. The changing business conditions also changed the interests of the executives; briefing books remained frozen as design formats. The traditional Executive Information System was not sufficient to meet an executive's future needs since he used data in a range of ways like referring to them for present use and analysing them for future needs. Executives had to follow the operating procedure in the organization. It was not possible to carry out one process until and unless others were ready. Today, the computer-based systems have solved those shortcomings by helping executives to take decisions on time.

Early EIS was a decision aid, specially designed for high-ranking managers in the organizations. It provided them with useful and most essential pieces of information for running their organization. Information overload is the phenomenon whereby the value of information creates additional burden. They required time to find out important information rather than to solve problems and make decisions. Unlike other decision tools, the EIS does not contain analytical models but only summarizes and consolidates data that are obtained from within the organization and the environment.

14.2 EXECUTIVE INFORMATION NEEDS

Executives have responsibilities and authority to delegate work to others. The executives have unique information needs. Mintzberg conducted a study of the information needs of executives. He identified five basic activities as follows:

- Desk work
- Telephone calls
- Unscheduled meetings
- Scheduled meetings
- Tours

He emphasized the role of the informal system. It had been found that the scheduled meetings cover around 59% of the total time. Deskwork was the next followed by unscheduled meetings. He did not work with computer-based information system, but his work had value considering the development of modern information system.

Another study by Mcleod and Professor Jack W. Jones saw a need to learn about EIS. The research was based on the value of information, source of information, media of communication, use of information and amount of information. According to the study, an executive received an average of 29 information transactions per day. There were considerable day-to-day variations in volume. The executives assigned values ranging from zero (no value) to tens (maximum value) to each transaction. There were also variations in the level of values assigned by each executive.

Computer-based information system has changed the value of information as the executive can develop the same based on his own requirements. For example, it is possible to organize mails and not to reply to irrelevant ones.

This study has given a picture of distribution of media to the executives. Again the computer-based system has taken over the maximum pie of the distribution. But still periodicals, memos, scheduled tours, meetings, etc. are also important sources of information. The research has also focused on how the executive is likely to use the information. Executives play different roles such as entrepreneur, disturbance handler, resource allocator and negotiator. Entrepreneur's role is most significant to an executive, which covers other roles as well. An executive runs business with many obligations towards society, government, employees and colleagues. In India, family-based business houses have been inducting more and more professional executives rather than family members. A renowned entrepreneur once said that the owner should not sit in the seat of Chief Executive Officer (CEO). But it is not true for all cases. The executive may not invest his own money, but generate resources or funds from different sources like banks, industrial houses and owner's equity banks, etc. As entrepreneurs, the executives generate resources and distribute those resources to run the business. They handle both internal and external customers. The organization runs under different set-ups. All public sector units do not run the business in the same operating procedure, even though in the same category like heavy electricals. The same executive may be transferred to different locations. The executive plays different roles to run the business under different needs. In each location, he works in the same position but his role is not the same. As a result, the information requirement is also different.

SPOTLIGHT

A company allows its employees to develop new products under the research and development department. The executive is required to submit the proposal to the board of directors. He prepares the report containing the details of the product to be developed, market potential, sales budget and even finance. All other respective departments support the executive to develop this proposal. Once the proposal is passed by the board of directors, the project is given to him for product development. He works with other team members to develop the product, as an entrepreneur. The success of the product goes to his account and he may become the chief executive for the product developed under him.

In this case, the executive works in an organizational set up where he can develop himself as an entrepreneur. The executive needs support services, when he plays the role of a negotiator. Departments prepare budget in the beginning of the financial year. All departments prepare the reports with data collected from other departments. Each department negotiates with other for the allocation of funds. In this situation, each executive plays the role of a negotiator.

The behavioural part is not discussed here. It is important to consider this aspect as an executive plays different roles in the organization.

14.3 COMPUTER-BASED EXECUTIVE INFORMATION SYSTEM

We will now discuss the computer-based executive information system.

Some discussions will be on non-computer-based EIS for the interest of the reader. But it is more pertinent to discuss the contemporary issues. Prior to EIS, it was common for executives to receive numerous fixed format reports, often hundreds of pages every month. The first computer-based system developed around 1980s was the mainframe system designed to replace paper, delivering the data on daily basis and not on weekly basis. EISs are useful to executives who often suffer from information overload. Top-level executive's decisions are based on highly summarized information. They review ratios of financial information, rather than account details, trial balance, etc. An executive first needs the general picture of a business situation. The executive could easily drill down from a piece of summary data down to lower and lower levels in order to get more details.

As discussed earlier, EIS does not contain any analytical model like DSS. It rather consolidates and summarizes data obtained from the sources outside and within the organization. Unlike a regular DSS, many EISs do not require the entering of the values of any parameters. The EIS is interfaced with the organizations' databases and data warehouses. An effective EIS has the following features:

(a) An easy-to-use user interface.
(b) An easy-to-learn graphics operation.
(c) Drill-down capability that allows the executive to reach information in greater depth.
(d) Sophisticated tools to allow navigation through the database.
(e) Inbuilt analysis tools.
(f) Access to external data pools.
(g) The ability to respond to ad hoc queries.

SPOTLIGHT

A customer support executive in a telephone service department received calls on excess billing from a customer. The billing generation process passes through following steps:

(a) The digital metre notes the number of telephone calls, which is the difference between the closing and opening metre balance for the month under consideration.
(b) This reading is checked for errors and signed by the respective divisional engineers.
(c) This checked report goes to accounts billing section for the generation of bills.
(d) The final bill is printed through a computer system and sent for distribution to customers.

In the above process, three departments namely divisional engineering, accounts and commercials are involved. Those departments are not linked together and are running independently using a computer-based information system. The customer's complaint goes to the customer service department. Then the bill passes through the commercial department to the engineering department and finally to the accounts department.

The drill-down facility is not available in this process as the system does not support it. Otherwise, the customer service executives could drill down to lower level to see the metre reading and correct it. The system then generates a new bill after the correction and hands over the same to the customer.

The system not only helps to solve an individual customer's problem, but also cater to special kinds of reports for decision-making.

Software is available in different functional areas of EIS. Organizations are more interested in customized products as EIS plays an important role in gaining a competitive advantage.

The cost of development of EIS is another major area for consideration. How does the Executive Support System (ESS) benefit managers? It is difficult to justify the cost of an EIS. Nevertheless, interest in this system is growing, so it is essential to examine the potential of EIS, put data and tools in the hands of executives who have to address specific problems. Executives are free to develop the solution to the problem, using the system as an extension of their own thinking processes.

The **visible benefits** of EIS are their ability to analyse, compare and highlight trends. The easy use of graphics allows the user to look at more data in shorter timeframes with greater clarity and insight. In the past, executives obtained the same information after days and weeks. The executives have freed themselves with the help of ESS.

ESS can change the working of the organization. The system allows decision-making to decentralize and to take place at the lower operating level. A well-defined ESS could dramatically improve the performance of the management and increase the upper management's span of control.

SPOTLIGHT

In a banking credit card service, customers can ask for any kind of information related to the credit card. The consumer service executive can drill down to any level of information and satisfy the customers in a very short span of time. He or she is authorized to take decisions at the point of service. The delegation of authority with the computer-based EIS has raised the customer's satisfaction to a higher level.

14.4 MANAGEMENT CHALLENGES

Building an information system is one of the challenges in EIS development. Critical success factors and other information requirement determination methods have been used so far for the successful implementation of EIS. It may still be difficult to establish information requirements for EIS. In many cases, as discussed earlier, the decisions are unstructured and fluid. It may be possible to address a problem with the help of an information system but a senior executive may fail to understand the needs. It is interesting to note that a company may be very successful in one region in running operations but fail to manage in the other region. It has been found that the flow of information may be same, though all may follow the same Standard Operating Procedure (SOP) but at the performance level the output varies. This is basically a psychological issue, where the mindset is much more important. The word "work culture" is the area of concern. The EIS people have been trying to overcome those issues by the implementation of computer-based information management.

The challenges faced by business houses due to environmental factors may not be possible to solve through the computer-based EIS. The myth about the computer is another barrier to the development of EIS. Failure to understand the computer-based information system causes a huge damage to the organization. Computer has its own limitations. For example, the E-commerce companies, namely, the dot-coms failed to understand the product or the customer or the both. The loss was immense and the impact long-term. Thus, the executives failed to analyse the situation.

Even if the system builders do know the information requirements, it may not be possible to fulfill them using data from the firm's existing information. It requires changes throughout the organization. The advancement of technology has helped the organization to develop the state-of-the-art information system management. ESS has been gaining academic importance all over the world. Some people use DSS and ESS interchangeably in many situations. The difference between DSS and ESS has blurred in recent years. Executives should look not at whether the system is labelled DSS or EIS, but take advantage of the different features offered.

REVIEW QUESTIONS

1. How do you define an executive?
2. What is an Executive Information System?
3. Can an Executive Information System be based on any software?
4. What do you understand by drill-down facility?
5. What are the challenges in designing an Executive Information System?
6. How are Decision Support System and Executive Information System linked together?
7. Can an Executive Information System be a part of Decision Support System?
8. How can an Executive Information System be useful to an executive?

DISCUSSION QUESTIONS

1. Executive Information Systems can change the organization. Discuss with examples.
2. What do you understand by a built-in-analyst tool?

15
Knowledge Management

15.1 INTRODUCTION

Knowledge is contextualized information enriched with individual interpretation and expertise, and that which can be applied. The origin is human mind. Basically, knowledge is of two types—either tacit or explicit. **Tacit knowledge** is composed of insights, perceptions, views, intuitions, hunches, observations, feelings, ideas, mental models, experiences, skills, reasoning and judgment. **Explicit knowledge** could be in the form of procedures, methodologies, business rules, case histories, observation reports, forecasts, predictions, design models, articles, product services, etc. **Knowledge** is a fluid of framed experience, values and contextual information that provides an environment and framework for evaluating and incorporating new experiences and information. In organizations, it often becomes embedded not only in documents but also in routines, processes, practices and norms. Basically, our main concern is the management of organizational knowledge for creating business value and generating a competitive advantage. Knowledge management is one of the challenges to the organization. The terms "knowledge economy", "knowledge workers", etc. are widely used by academics. Unfortunately there is no universal definition of knowledge management. It is best to think of knowledge management in the broadest context. Succinctly put, knowledge management is a process through which an organization generates value for its intellectual and knowledge-based assets. Often generating value from such assets involves sharing them among employees, departments even with competitors in an effort to device best practices.

An overarching theory of knowledge management has yet to emerge, perhaps because the practices associated with managing knowledge have their roots in a variety of disciplines and domains. By the mid of 1980s, the importance of knowledge as a competitive asset was apparent even though the classical economic theory ignores knowledge as an asset and most organizations still lack strategies and methods for managing it. Now the area of concern is how to deal with the exponential increase in the amount of available knowledge and increasingly complex products and processes. The computer technology that has contributed so heavily to superabundance of information, started to become a part of the solution in a variety of domains.

In another way, knowledge management is the explicit and systematic management of vital knowledge and its associated processes of creating, gathering, organizing, diffusion and exploitation. It requires turning personal knowledge into corporate knowledge that can be widely shared throughout an organization and can be appropriately applied. Not all information is valuable. Therefore, it is up to the individual company to determine what information qualifies as intellectual and knowledge-based assets. In general, however, intellectual and knowledge-based assets fall into two categories: explicit and tacit. Knowledge management is a dynamic issue. Information plays a very vital role in the knowledge economy. The basic question is why do we need knowledge management? Some of the specific factors include:

(a) Market places are increasingly competitive and innovation is continuous.
(b) Reduction in employee strength creates a need to replace informal knowledge with formal methods.
(c) The time available to experience and acquire knowledge has diminished.
(d) Organizations compete on knowledge base.
(e) There is a need to manage increasing complexity, as small operating companies are transnational sourcing operations.
(f) Products and services are increasingly complex, endowing them with a significant information component.

The change has been taking place globally. Companies are customer focused and at the same time customers are educated enough on products and services.

Knowledge management needs to be inculcated in the organization. It is a culture to be developed over time. The key word is "learning organization". This means the process of creating, acquiring, sharing and applying knowledge to achieve better results. The major problem that occurs in knowledge management usually is companies' reluctance to accept tacit knowledge. It requires a culture, which recognizes tacit knowledge and encourages employees to share it. The tacit knowledge makes an individual valuable to the organization.

Knowledge management is not a technology, nor a software solution. Do not be duped by software vendors touting their knowledge management solution. Technology can support knowledge management but it is not the starting point of the knowledge management programme.

A knowledge management programme should always be linked with business objective. While sharing of best practices is a commendable idea, there must be an underlying business reason to do so. Knowledge management is an exercise in futility without knowledge.

Knowledge can erode over time. The relevance of knowledge at any given point of time changes, as do the skills of employees. Therefore, there is no endpoint to a knowledge management programme. Like other kind of developments, knowledge management is a constantly evolving business practice. Companies need to be diligent and on the look out for information over load. Quality and quantity rarely equals, and knowledge management is no exception. The organization should focus on knowledge management programme to identify and disseminate knowledge gems from the sea of information.

So it is more important to create the awareness throughout the organization. Innovation takes a major role as it helps making the transition from ideas to commercialization more effective. It is recommended to share existing knowledge, making implicit knowledge more explicit and applying more rapidly to where it is needed.

Knowledge management programmes typically have one or more of the following activities:

- Knowledge leader is to be appointed to promote the agenda.
- A knowledge team creation with members from all disciplines.
- Develop knowledge bases—best practices, market intelligence.
- Active process-management.
- Development of knowledge centres.
- Creation of intellectual capital teams.
- Network of experts, who collaborate across divisions.
- Participation in programmes that encourage knowledge exchange.

15.2 MANAGING KNOWLEDGE AND KNOWLEDGE WORKERS

Knowledge management is a general term applied to almost any functional area of an organization. It is designed to preserve, transfer or exploit knowledge from one part of the organization to another. All organizations are already involved in knowledge management but often it is done implicitly and informally. The formal way of managing knowledge is simply to make knowledge-market places to operate more efficiently. Today, knowledge is another way of money. Organizations recognize that ownership of knowledge is the key competitive differentiation. Lack of knowledge management programmes is another way of losing opportunities. Either the organizations are unable to find the knowledge they need, or they make decisions based on inadequate information.

The implementation and institutionalisation of knowledge management in organizations usually faces many hurdles.

(1) **Introversion:** Avoid to learn from an outsider or do not expose internal operations to others, namely customers. It may be an individual or a group in the organization. It deals with the cultural aspect of the organization.

(2) **Lack of top management involvement:** Most often, top management is busy with day-to-day affairs. It is not possible to institutionalize values and norms and create organizational culture, until and unless the top management is cooperative.

(3) **Organizational structure hindering learning:** Hierarchies hinder information flow from lower level to higher level. It is interesting to note that even in flatter organizations, knowledge sharing does not occur easily. It has been found that knowledge workers are reluctant to learn from and to share information with their colleagues.

(4) **Lack of organizational strategy:** Knowledge management should have strong linkage with organizational strategy. It should facilitate unique competencies of the people in the organization. The information technology should be effectively utilized for knowledge sharing and knowledge generation. The biggest challenge is that of changing the culture from "knowledge is power" to "knowledge sharing is power".

(5) **Organizational recognition and reward system:** Usually a reward system focuses on only tangible and quick results. Reward systems usually do not sufficiently recognize knowledge contribution. They are linked to traditional financial measures. Discretionary rewards being big, everyone in the organization becomes conscious about performance criteria. It leads to tangible, visible and objective results. In comparison, the knowledge management process is not easily visible and subjective in some of the cases, and hence the reward system becomes dysfunctional for knowledge sharing and knowledge generation.

(6) **Treating it as one-off project or quick-win programme:** Knowledge management is a commitment to the long-term and the future prosperity of the organization. It goes beyond the limit of any single function or discipline. All functions must collaborate.

Now knowledge generation is the area under consideration. The first objective of knowledge management is to create awareness throughout the organization.

Several researches have identified a number recurring success factors, for knowledge generation in the organization. They are as follows:

(a) **Organizations require a knowledge leader or champion:** Someone who actively drives the knowledge agenda forward creates enthusiasm and commitment.
(b) **A clear value proposition:** It provides the identification of the link between knowledge and the bottom line business benefit, new measures of performance and appropriate rewards.
(c) **A compelling vision and architecture:** This is a framework that drives the agenda forward.
(d) Creation of a culture through the organization that supports innovation, learning and knowledge sharing. This is usually supported by appropriate reward mechanisms.
(e) An information technology based infrastructure that supports knowledge work. In other words, from simple, knowledge support tools to sophisticated decision support systems.
(f) Development of system knowledge process, supported by specialists in an information management with close partnership between users and providers of information.

Knowledge workers are essential for day-to-day organizational work. Software companies, especially software development, deal with knowledge workers. Research organizations, research and development within an organization, banks, pharmaceutical companies and service companies have been managing knowledge workers. The key discussion points are the characteristics of knowledge workers and how to retain them in organizations.

Following are the characteristics of a knowledge worker:

(a) Knowledge workers invest time, efforts and resources to acquire relevant and valid knowledge.
(b) Knowledge workers like to apply their existing knowledge and prefer to work under environment which provides opportunities for knowledge generation.
(c) Knowledge workers are high achievers and they expect recognition for their performances.
(d) Knowledge workers are more committed to their profession rather than to organizations.
(e) Due to high demand, they are able to move from one organization to another.
(f) Knowledge workers are professional, innovative and self-starters.

It is quite clear from the discussion that the knowledge workers are in high demand. It has far more lasting effects in the long run. As an organization grows, it generates a culture of knowledge generation throughout the organization. As a result, it attracts more knowledge workers. It is a spiral effect, which helps organization to attract the best quality workers in the long run.

Knowledge organizations which are interested in attracting and retaining knowledge workers would require to ensure that they offer excellent environment for knowledge generation. The organization should ensure and encourage knowledge workers to examine their beliefs through the knowledge sharing process. Organization should select knowledge workers based on their capabilities to learn and evidences for the desire to learn. Existing knowledge workers are needed to be involved in selecting, maintaining, and training new knowledge workers. Overall, the approach has to be whole and spread throughout the organization. Organizations should design reward systems for knowledge management. Knowledge generation, knowledge usage, knowledge acquisition and knowledge retention activities are intrinsically motivating and satisfying for a knowledge worker. These activities generate self-knowledge within the organization. Thus, organizations should invest time and resources to recruit superior knowledge workers. Organizations should develop a culture to communicate organizational values though knowledge generation and sharing. Thus organizations need to nurture knowledge worker communities, which in turn, become reference groups for their knowledge workers. Organizations should encourage their knowledge workers to benchmark and share knowledge with other institutions.

15.3 KNOWLEDGE MANAGEMENT IN ELECTRONIC BUSINESS

Information strategy executives observed some significant transitions during the last quarter of the 20th century. In the new world of business, most enterprises' success or failure would depend upon their ability to incessantly question and change business models and business processes and introduce sustained dynamic and radical changes in the business environment.

E-business companies have been doing business through internet. It has given birth to online communities all over the world. Recent developments in World Wide Web-based collaborative technologies are being heralded as the enablers of the knowledge-based enterprise in E-business. The role of online communities has become increasingly important in the success of E-business. Commercial success of E-business depends on organizing and exploiting the potential of virtual enterprises. Their success is based on the premise that knowledge, content and resources produced by online communities are extremely valuable commodities. Customers are demanding more specialized products, which automatically leads to a broader product range that companies have to develop and produce. E-business sites offer many products to the customer. The business model may look same for similar products and services. But the underlying strategy may be different and difficult to replicate in business. Companies have to tailor their products and services, resulting in increasing complexity across all organizational functions.

In E-business model, the knowledge management process is quite different from the traditional concepts. The exchange of information is vital for virtual corporations. A virtual corporation may not be feasible without information technology. Virtual organizations work with partners, without consideration of the boundary.

> **SPOTLIGHT**
>
> A company sells products like CDs, pendrives, etc. through internet. The company outsources the merchandise through different manufacturers. Once the order is received via internet, the order is generated for bulk and sent to the manufacturers for supplying the product to the logistic service provider. The logistic service partner delivers the product to the consumer addresses given by the company. Company, in turn, receives the payment by credit card via internet.

The above example shows that partners play a major role in the success of the business. Partners like logistic service providers and banks come across direct customers. Each partner has its own database to communicate with customers. Since it is boundary free, the knowledge management process becomes more complicated over time. The model-based on trust within the network partners. One of the major problems of E-business companies is the search of suitable partner companies; companies which fit together in terms of mutual trust, organizational culture, business process and information communication systems.

The discussion highlights the dual nature of knowledge management. Knowledge management by design is characterized by pre-determination, pre-specification and programming for knowledge. On the other hand, knowledge management by emergence is characterized by the creation of cultural infrastructure, which enables continuous knowledge sharing, knowledge renewal and knowledge creation.

The partners work under this network with their own infrastructure. So, the emergence characteristics of knowledge management are visible under this E-business model. The job of the knowledge management is to maintain and develop those characteristics in the long run. Knowledge management by design is applicable in areas of relatively high structure routinisation of processes and tasks, and business environment which is stable. This is the area that represents automation of processes using smart technologies and rationalization to streamline workflows and reengineering of business processes to achieve the highest level of efficiency. The organization works with partners. It involves high risk as the companies try to morph their internal and external value chains. The E-business customers provide their own data through internet. The question-answer information exchange helps to gather more information about customers. In the process, the organization exchanges more complex knowledge deliverables like integrated pricing, bidding, reverse-auction mechanism, etc. Organization can use knowledge exchange for the high-end deliverables. Such knowledge deliverables include more complex research on knowledge management practice. It is all about collaboration of efforts to manage data by many vendors.

The exchange process develops the database on a long-term basis, which in turn helps organizations in carrying out further research on data. Such collaborative systems for specifying, refining, matchmaking, rating, pricing are evolving along with systems that would allow rapid execution of such deliverables. In other words, those deliverables are tacit knowledge in nature. The free e-mail is a setback on knowledge management in electronic market (E-market). The dot-com hype had burst because they misunderstood the deliverables. The implicit part is manageable through technology under different conditions. But the tacit part is more important in collaborative efforts.

Many emerging models of knowledge exchange represent harbingers of extra-organizational collaborations, which will be required for the execution of the organizational knowledge work. There is an utmost need for understanding how knowledge management can be developed through collaborative technology application, which is necessary for the renewal of the existing knowledge as well as creation of new knowledge.

REVIEW QUESTIONS

1. What do you understand by Knowledge Management?
2. How does Knowledge Management relate to organization culture?
3. Why do we need Knowledge Management?
4. List the activities involved in Knowledge Management.
5. What are the barriers that an organization faces in Knowledge Management?
6. How do you define a knowledge worker?
7. How is Knowledge Management useful in E-business?
8. How do you manage the database in Knowledge Management?
9. What is tacit knowledge?
10. What do you understand by explicit knowledge?

DISCUSSION QUESTIONS

1. Knowledge Management is not a technology. Establish this statement with examples.

2. A Knowledge Management program is always linked with the business objective. Explain with examples.
3. How do you define the ownership of knowledge? How can it play a useful role in gaining competitive advantage?
4. Knowledge workers are not job satisfied. Do you agree with this statement and why?

16

Information Systems: Ethical and Social Issues

16.1 ETHICAL AND SOCIAL ISSUES

Corporate culture should reinforce the strategy and structural design that help an organization to be effective within its environment of cultural and ethical values and now this aspect is considered as one among the most important things. Ethical standards are becoming part of the formal policies and informal culture of many organizations. Ethics is the code of moral principles and values that governs the behaviour of a person or a group with respect to what is right or wrong. Ethics is distinct from behaviours governed by law. The rule of law arises from a set of codified principles and regulations which describe how people are required to act. Law is generally accepted in society and is enforceable in the courts. Ethical standards, for the most part, apply to behaviours not covered by law.

Unethical conduct in organizations is surprisingly widespread. Many people feel and believe that if you are not breaking the law, then you are behaving in an ethical manner, but ethics is much more than law. Managerial ethics are principles that guide the decisions and behaviours of managers in the organization.

An individual brings a set of personal beliefs and values into the workplace. It is very rare that ethical or unethical business practices are attributed entirely to the personal ethics of a single individual. As business practice reflects the organizational culture, ethics is an organizational issue here. It is not possible to stop individual perception with respect to organization.

Over the years, technology has given different shapes to society. Each invention such as steam engine, electricity, internal combustion engine, telephone, radio etc. offered new opportunities for social changes and individual actions. Information technology is certainly not the first technology to offer the potential for radical social changes. The new technology threatens the existing distribution of money, power, rights and obligations. The development of information technology will produce gainers and losers, will produce benefits for many and costs for others. Implementation of information technology, in most industrial societies, helped to reduce the work from 60 hours to around 40 hours. Technology is not just an outside event; it produces profound influence but acting upon society.

An individual has a right to share and distribute or to deliver information to the organization. The organization supports an individual or a group to implement actions. Information technology is one of the helping tools to take the decisions. Thus, individuals have information rights and obligations to the organization. In another way, they are concerned with property rights. Other factors that have been playing critical roles are system quality and quality of life. It is true that information technology has improved the productivity of the organizations. At the same time, our vulnerability to the system errors and poor data quality have also increased. Occasional failures of the system are of concern due to growing dependence on critical systems. The database is the root of any business. The customer database is available and stored in different media. The data storage methods have increased the routine violations of organization privacy to such resources.

The internet has opened up new dimensions to business. It has given birth to information society. Its impact is widespread in society. The internet is not only the repository of data but also replete with many technological tools. The internet has reached a certain height today that it is quite difficult to be managed by an individual. Free e-mail is another kind of public property. The law cannot be enforced against an individual who misuses the internet.

Computer crime can be defined as the commission of illegal acts through the use of a computer. A computer system can became an instrument of a crime. In the same way, accessing a computer without authorization, or with intention to do harm is a crime. It is one of the most difficult tasks to find out the magnitude of the computer crimes. Many organizations are reluctant to report computer crimes, for they may lose their market.

SPOTLIGHT

The system administrator works on the e-mail server, where the mails are stored. The company follows a policy where they check e-mails of employees occasionally. Employees may not be aware of this and as a matter of policy this practice is not disclosed to them. An individual employee may feel that he has every right to use his e-mail account and should not be under the vigil of the company. On the other hand, the company feels that the employees should not misuse the e-mail service. As a matter of fact, expenditure is incurred by the organization for the e-mail account.

16.2 ETHICS AND MORAL DIMENSIONS

In a society, an individual plays different roles. Organizations run under different social, political, and ethical stands. The moral dimension of information system deals with different angles. Information right is one of the issues under moral dimensions. When should be one allowed to invade the privacy of others? What legitimizes the intrusion into other's privacy? Privacy and freedom in information society is one dimension. Privacy is the claim of individuals to be left alone and free of interference from others. The senior employee may be authorized to delegate his responsibility to juniors, but the Standard Operating Procedure (SOP) may not allow this. It all depends on the culture of the organization.

In the same manner, the information passed to others in the organization needs to be fair and correct. Fair information practice principles are based on the notion of mutuality of interest between the record holder and the individual. The individual maintains a record and the record may not be used to support other activities without the consent of individuals. Freedom in information society has been passing through different dimensions. The internet is the latest debate in information freedom. It is literally difficult to maintain fair information over the internet.

Fair information practice principles state that a government has the right to intervene in the information relationship. In internet, it may not be possible to maintain fair information practices since its spread is throughout the world.

The second issue is the intellectual property. Knowledge management is a burning topic today. The piracy is very common in information technology. There is a loss of billions of dollars in software sales due to outright theft or piracy and the consequent retarded growth of the industry. Any intellectual output—formula, pattern, software program, compiled database—used for a business purpose can be classified as trade secrets. Software programs which contain procedures, unique key features, etc. are trade secrets. The program should not come under the public domain. The trade secrets provide competitive business advantages, using the less well-known techniques. The key is to avoid having ideas fall into public domain.

Copyright is a statutory provision which protects the creators of intellectual property against copying by others for any purpose without the written permission of the copyright holders. Most industrial nations have their copyright laws. Copyright protection is explicit and clear-cut. It protects against copying of entire program or part of the program. Books, study materials are available in CDs. Specially designed study materials are interactive. Companies producing those materials are protected by copyright.

A patent grants the owner an exclusive monopoly on the ideas behind inventions. The key concept of patent is originality, novelty and invention. The strength of the patent lies in the monopoly. In information technology, the equipment plays another major role. For example, printers of different types, scanners, web cameras, modems are manufactured by different companies. Assembled machines, on the other hand, marketed by unscrupulous traders are less costly. The industry has been fighting against the assembled components for many years.

Contemporary information technology poses a severe challenge to knowledge management, which in turn, is a challenge to intellectual property. Digital media allows replication, transmission and alteration in a very sophisticated way. It is very difficult distinguish between the original and a pirated product. Organizational values play a major role. Companies are offering free source codes to consumers. Free downloadable software are available on the internet. Computer piracy is a common threat throughout the industry. The internet also has given birth to new threats; yesteryears, computer virus was not so common. But free access to the internet is injecting virus into machines more easily. Internet itself is a local problem for other areas. Payment, purchase via internet has been gaining market throughout the world. The protection of the consumer is not available though any proper law even today. Here again, the intruder may break the password and use the credit card of the consumer. The society itself needs to be trained via media as technology is upgraded. It is more important to develop society, which in turn, contributes to the organizational development.

SPOTLIGHT

A software product is not easily purchased if it is not worthwhile. The common thing is to pirate due to the high cost of the product or if it is not useful enough for a long period. The software development companies now prefer to offer a 30-days evaluation copy free of cost with most of the features of the original software in it. The customers have the option not to purchase the software if not satisfied after the evaluation of the same. On the other hand, they may ask for some upgradation, modification of the product with extra cost or buy it after the stipulated time of 30 days. This offer is designed by the software development companies to discourage piracy. On the other hand, the non-free nature of the product restrict users from distributing or to copying them for others.

16.3 MANAGEMENT CHALLENGES

Business, government, schools, private associations are depending heavily on information technology. The information technology is running the back-end of many services like, telephone, radio, television and other public utility services. An information system is not a utility. Society has been reshaping itself through the information overflow because in many cases, technology has been playing a major role in developing countries. Economies are much more sanguine about the potential job losses. Knowledge economy demands bright educated workers from re-engineered jobs to better jobs for the initial growth of industries. Left out of this are old, less educated middle level managers. It is not clear that this group can be easily trained for quality jobs. On the other hand, the labour force has increased because of women and participation of minority groups. Careful planning, and sensitivity to employee needs can help companies redesign work to minimize job losses.

The next challenge is health risk. The most popular occupational disease of today is Repetitive Stress Injury (RSI). RSI occurs for the following reasons:

(a) Muscles are stressed due to the repetitive actions involving high impact loads.
(b) Repetition under low impact loads.

The second problem deals with working at a computer keyboard. RSI in the computer field is carpal tunnel syndrome. This is caused by constant repetition of keystrokes. The treatment of RSI is expensive. The workers should not blame the company. It is possible to overcome RSI. New types of keyboards have been designed to overcome RSI.

Computer vision syndrome refers to the eye strain caused by monitors. Its symptoms are usually headache, irritated eyes, blurred vision, etc.

Another area of concern is techno stress. It has many psychological impacts, such as impatience, aggravation, enervation, etc. A study shows that a human being working with computer, continuously expects others to behave like a computer, ignoring emotions. Even management may not consider the problems attributable to use of computer. But computer related jobs are now on the top of the list of stressful occupations.

The debate over liability and responsibility of unintentional consequences of information systems is another area under study. The software product developed by others is installed in hardware. The liability cames under question when the hardware fails or breaks down. This situation may cause a loss of reasonable amount of time and money. In the case of a public utility service, the damage may be enormous. The source of problem may be software bugs and errors, hardware or facility failure due to other causes. So, the user must be aware of the probability for catastrophic failures. It is not possible to standardize the process. For life-saving applications, further protective measures are possible. The responsibility should not be passed from one machine manufacturer to another or to the product developer. The hardware product has to run through the software product. Thus quality factor is another important part. The software developers should know at what point in time the software is to be released with adequate level of technical quality.

The internet is a repository of data. E-mail is one of the cheapest products of communication. The free e-mail account is another threat to organizations. Junk mail is a real problem under any account. Free e-mail is a public domain. So, in case of misuse, it may not be easy to catch hold of the culprit. Another threat is the prevalence of pornographic sites and this could be a major threat in the future until and unless countries all over the world join together to solve this problem.

SPOTLIGHT

> The password is a very common term in computer software. Any software protected by a password is available only to the user. The organization's password is known to one or more persons. It is required to be available to some people for smooth functioning of organization. The information should not be accessible to unauthorized employees. This, however, generates mistrust within the organization on this delicate issue of password.

The culture of the organization plays a major role in ethical issues. The results could be disastrous of the system, depending on functional areas or applications.

REVIEW QUESTIONS

1. Describe the ethical issues that may arise in any organization.
2. What do you understand by computer crime?
3. What is intellectual property?
4. What is computer piracy?
5. What do you understand by fair information practices?
6. Explain the term patent.

DISCUSSION QUESTIONS

1. Individuals have the right to share and deliver information to the organization. Give your views.
2. Do you feel that free software can stop computer piracy?
3. What are the moral dimensions involved in Information Systems?

Appendix

Case I
HOTEL IS HOT

The hotel Subhalaxmi is situated on the outskirts of the city where it has no competitors. The place is of some historical interest. The government has set up one university campus on forty acres of land. The university offers courses on foreign languages in addition to traditional streams. The hotel is about two kilometres away from the university and about five kilometers from the nearest railway station. The place is renowned for some special events, where people come from all over the country to attend these events. Normally they stay four to five days and thrice a year on different occasions. In addition, travellers come here during weekends from different parts of the state.

Subhalaxmi is a three-star hotel with a swimming pool, a bar and an open air restaurant. It has ten non-AC and twenty AC double rooms. It has one banquet hall which can accommodate 200 guests. There is a restaurant inside to serve lunch and dinner to its boarders. The hotel has one city-booking office for advance booking. The hotel also has corporate customers who can avail discounts for their employees. The hotel also offers other services, such as laundry, doctor-on-call, swimming pool, and video parlour, etc.

All rooms are connected via an EPABX system. The checkout time is 1 pm and the bills are settled at reception.

The reception has one computer. It stores data related to the customer, i.e. name, address, and check-in time, date of booking, room type, and requests for different services. The customers are provided with a computer printout of their bill at the time of checkout.

The customers have to wait a long at the time of checkout. It takes at least one hour to release a customer at the time of checkout. Since customers make use of different services, they cannot settle the final bill until and unless all the bills reach the reception. Laundry, medicine shop, video parlour, etc. prepare bills manually and send to reception at the time of checkout. Each department takes minimum twenty to thirty minutes to settle the bill. It has been found that the bills prepared by the reception also carry the following mistakes:

(1) Incorrect billing information from different departments.
(2) Restaurant bills carry mistakes on the price of the items offered.
(3) In some cases, bill is also prepared for some services which are not availed by the customer.
(4) Discount is wrongly calculated for the corporate customers.
(5) Phone bills are incorrect in most of the cases. Sometimes a bill is prepared even for a customer who has not made a single call.
(6) Bill total also carries mistakes.

The hotel also faces another problem; when booking is done from the city office, in some cases, information is not available on the details of booking and cancellation. The end result is that the customers do not receive the type of room they actually booked, or the room remains unused owing to the cancellation information being not available on time.

The management of the hotel is concerned about these problems. A new hotel has opened in the same area with similar facilities. The Subhalaxmi hotel has been losing customers since last year. They have approached a consultancy firm to solve this problem. The firm started working with individual departments and met some customers as well. The consultancy firm studied all the systems, processes, etc. of the hotel for four months and submitted a report to the management with the following findings and recommended solutions.

(a) Reception should use the computer to manage the information properly. The existing software does not allow to input many services with detailed information. For example, the software package allows to enter only the total amount of laundry bills, but not the amounts on a daily basis.
(b) The restaurant bill is prepared manually and hence is susceptible to mistakes.
(c) In the early morning and late at night, there are no attendants in swimming pool, video parlour and reception.
(d) The customer has to come to reception for making external phone calls. The machine cannot print the name of the customer, so the phone bills often get misplaced.
(e) The reception does not maintain a logbook to record the daily services availed by a customer. They compile all that information at the time of checkout.
(f) The city office often fails to send all the booking details to the hotel on time.
(g) The reception is open from 6 am to 8 pm. No body is responsible to maintain data after these hours and the result is information lapses.

The consultancy firm found out that the information management was the main area of concern. They recommended solutions to the hotel in different functional areas.

Questions

1. In your opinion, what were the problems of the hotel?
2. Can you suggest some measures to solve those problems?

Case II
SOFTWARE IS SOFT

Bigboy Finance Co. (Pvt.) Ltd. is a medium size Kolkata-based finance company. The primary business dealings are buying and selling of shares, hire purchase and bill discounting, intercorporate deposits, etc. The total staff strength is ten. They follow the manual system for all jobs. The company then decided to introduce computers in the organization with accounting software and document management software.

The company buys shares from the stock exchange and sells them to stock market and individual buyers. The company also deals in intercorporate deposits of companies which are performing well in the stock market. Bill discounting and hire purchase contribution is small in the total pie chart. The accounting and tax are two areas having maximum loads. Stock of shares is maintained manually, and checking is done at the time of delivery. Tax is another area of concern. They pay tax on shares—on short-term and long-term shares. In the short term, which is of one year, they pay tax on profit. But in the long-term shares, the process is different, which needs special attention. The government publishes the share index each year to calculate the cost of the shares for the long term. The basic concept is that the cost of purchase of the shares cannot be the same always. So, the index allows to find out the price of the shares for calculating profit, which, in turn, is taxable. The company maintains their transactions manually.

The CEO decided to:

(a) Buy two computers
(b) Buy one accounting software package and office automation software
(c) One printer

The company then recruited one person to handle computers. The accounting package allows to enter all transaction data such as bank, cash, sale, purchase journal voucher, etc. It, however, cannot calculate the long-term or short-term profit. The profit on selling of shares is calculated with the help of spreadsheet and the same data is entered in the accounting package. The company has come out with a problem; the accounting software is not useful to them, and hence requires modifications.

While using the readymade accounting package, the user has to define the supplier and the customer in the beginning, i.e. the name of the supplier needs to be entered before the starting entry on this account. The package does not allow two accounts in the name of the same supplier. The business of the company is to buy and to sell shares. They buy shares from a broker, who act as a supplier, and when they sell, the package treats the broker as a customer. A broker can be a buyer and seller at the same time. But the software package requires two different accounts for the same broker. The company needs to have two ledger accounts to see the balance of the broker, which affects the whole decision-making process of the company as it has around 30–35 stockbrokers.

The company, therefore, approached the vendor who had developed the package, but the cost of customization was too high. So, the company decided to run the same accounting package for another financial year.

Next year, having gained more experience on accounting software and computerization practices, the company approached a dealer to manage stock trading. In the same year, the company applied to National Stock Exchange for approval to act as a broker. The new package was installed which can also calculate the short- and long-term profit with index. So, the company stopped maintaining the spreadsheet job.

The second wave came after the company got approval from the National Stock Exchange. The National Stock Exchange distributes software packages to run with their national network. All information was submitted beforehand, but the company failed to understand the implication. The new broker management package did not allow import of National Stock Exchange data. So, for the transactions through the National Stock Exchange, the company had to maintain a separate account. A customer may exist in both the cases. The solution was not available immediately. It needed immediate attention.

The CEO was confused. He felt that the experience and knowledge was more important to select a solution on computerization. He could not rely on the new software vendors. So, he decided to talk to a computer consultant to solve the bottleneck.

Questions

1. Can you recommend a solution to the CEO as a consultant?
2. Do you think that the CEO handled the situation effectively?

Case III
ORGANIZATION: CAN YOU ORGANIZE?

VOIP Ltd. is a company manufacturing industrial valves for the oil sector. The company has its head office in the city with accounts, finance, marketing, and administration personnel totalling about 45 employees. The factory has three set-ups: accounts and costing, sales, and production. The factory has three segments where facilities are available. They have one main building from where accounts, HR, sales and communication personnel operate. The store is hundred metres away from the main building, near the workshop. The head office or the city office is around sixty kilometres away from the factory. Commuting facility is available to those employees who come from city. The factory has employees' quarters within one kilometre of the factory premises.

The company's capital is financed by a consortium of banks. The bank consortium has also its nominee on the Board of Directors. The following figure represents the hierarchy of the organization:

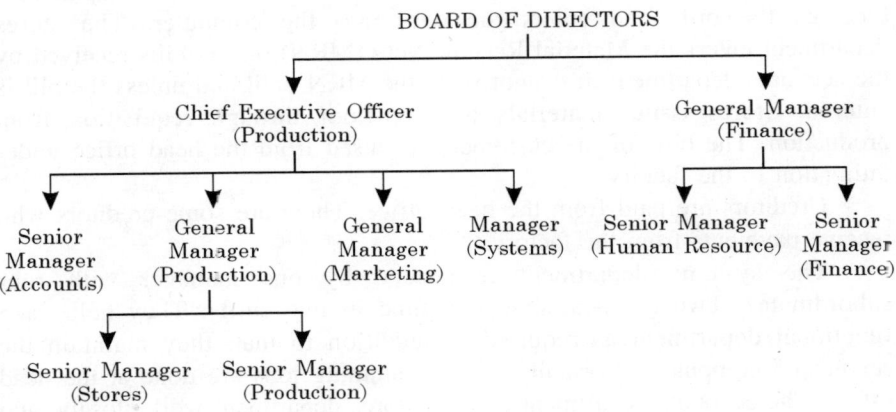

The communication to the head office and factory is via telephones. The documents are delivered by the company vehicle daily. The CEO looks after both the places and the General Manager (Finance) is normally available at the head office. The head office is connected with Local Area Network (LAN); 16 computers are connected with the server. The director also has access to the network. They have Window NT server with ERP software solution as for a medium size company. They also have other office automation equipment, such as fax, e-mail, photocopier, security system, etc. The finance department works in liaison with the bank consortium.

The factory is connected to 40 computers with two Window NT servers. One server deals with the same ERP software that is available at head office, the other one deals with attendance, quality control in shop-floor, and design and drawing. The accounts department is headed by a

Senior Manager (Accounts), who is a cost accountant by profession. He has around twenty-two years of experience in manufacturing industry. Four persons work under him with three nodes available to them. The stores department works very closely with the accounts department. The store has two computers. Each month, preferably in the first week, the accounts department sends a report to the head office on accounts details, which in turn go to the bank consortium. The working capital loan is financed by the bank consortium and this consortium requires the following pieces of information:

(a) Outstanding sundry debtors
(b) Outstanding sundry creditors
(c) Stock details
(d) Other documents.

The documents are generated at the factory based on the raw data available there. The supplier submits the bills to the purchase department in head office with a delivery challan. They send the materials to the factory stores and the original bill to factory accounts. The accounts department receives the bills and enters the data into the computer. The stores department enters the Material Receipt Note (MRN) on the bills received by the accounts department. It cannot issue the MRN until and unless the bill is entered. Stores issues materials to shop-floor through requisition from production. The bills of the customer are raised from the head office under intimation to the factory.

Creditors are paid from the head office. There are some creditors who receive payments from the factory.

The systems department is headed by one manager with four subordinates. Two are available at a time in two shifts. They help each functional department as required. In addition to that, they maintain the server and computers. Normally all programming jobs are done at the head office. The accounts department and the stores department work closely, and in the last week of each month, they require special support from the systems department.

The reports are submitted to the bank on the 15th of each month. The bank dealings on loans are based on the reports. The bank charges interest on the loan amount and charges two per cent penalty if the report is not submitted on time. So the head office requires the reports from factory accounts at least seven days before it is due for submission to the bank.

The company has been facing a typical problem for the last six months. Often the report is not ready or incomplete or full of mistakes. As the General Manager (Finance) and Senior Manager (Systems) have joined very recently (both joined three months ago), the bank brought this issue to their notice. Bank has also sent a note to them explaining the failure status. General Manager (Finance) sent a note to the Factory Manager (Finance) to find out the reason for delay and other problems. Factory Manager (Finance) sent the following memo.

INTERNAL MEMO

To: General Manager (Finance)   From: Senior Manager (Accounts)

Date:

The problem is due to the improper working of the computer system. The data are not saved by the software, which resulted in further data entry of the same, thus delaying the job. Computers in the stores department have been lying dead for the last four months and not repaired even after several reminders. The mistakes in the reports are due to the problems in the software. Your reply in this regard is solicited.

The General Manager (Finance) replied and a copy was sent to the Manager (Systems) asking for a clarification. The reply memo from Manager (Systems) is as follows:

INTERNAL MEMO

To: General Manager (Finance)   From: Manager (Systems)

The system has been studied for one week. It has been observed that the data are not entered on time. The accounts department does not enter the bills daily. So the stores department could not enter the MRNs. As a result, the stock is not updated and the production issues wrong requisitions. The servers are handled by others in the absence of the system administrator, which is not correct.

General Manager (Finance) was not comfortable with the situation. He spent four days at the factory to look into the matter personally. It came to his notice that the accounts department had been making unnecessary delays in the data entry, which in turn affected the stores department.

The rumour in the office was that the General Manager (Finance) favoured the Manager (Systems) as both of them joined newly. The CEO was not interested in discussions as he felt them unimportant. The CEO directed that the next date of submission of report to the bank must be maintained to avoid penalty.

Questions

1. List the nature of the problem encountered in this case by the organization?
2. How does the CEO solve the problem?
3. Do you think there is any conflict between the different departments of the organization?

Case IV
SUPPLY CHAIN MANAGEMENT
A Pharmaceutical Company

Mr. Manish, the General Manager (Warehouse) was discussing his plan of outbound logistics, which had been developed and implemented under his leadership. The model had been developed by his team named Global Supply Chain (GSC) group. An M.Pharm from Mumbai University and an MBA from Jamunalal Bajaj Institute of Management, Mr. Manish had started his career with Nicol. Later he spent 7 years with a small pharmaceutical company, where he gained further experience in pharmaceutical business in India. In the year 1988, he joined Totman as a quality control manager. Today as a GM (Warehouse), he looks after GSC with three senior managers under him.

Background

Totman Limited is today well positioned in its quest to become a research-based international pharmaceutical company. Totman Limited is amongst the top pharmaceutical companies in India. The company exports its products to over 20 countries with offices in 25 cities outside India and manufacturing facilities in four countries.

Growing at a rate of around 20 per cent in sales in the last decade, Totman Limited is a progressive and quality conscious multinational organization serving the pharmaceutical needs of diverse markets around the globe comprising developing, emerging and advanced countries. Totman Limited attributes its phenomenal growth to the vitality, innovation and commitment of its over 2000-strong multicultural workforce. In the quest to become international, the importance of a solid home foundation cannot be overlooked.

Totman Limited enjoys an enviable reputation amongst the medical fraternity for its high standards of ethics and quality. Around the core strength of its antibiotics, where some of the best recognized brands have led over decades, the company has built more core areas recently in the emerging therapeutic fields such cardio-vascular, central nervous system and nutritional supplements that reflect lifestyle transitions. As the company fortifies its presence further in this market, it is turning the Indian learning into an international opportunity.

Using the finest research and development and manufacturing facilities, Totman Limited manufactures and markets generic pharmaceuticals, value added generic pharmaceuticals, branded generics, Active Pharmaceuticals and Intermediates (API).

The company remains focused on ascending the value chain in the marketing of pharmaceutical substances and is determined to bring in increased revenues from sales.

Totman's drive for internationalization is guided by a well-planned brand strategy. The company has over 15 global brands in its basket which will strengthen its position in international market.

Manufacturing

The manufacturing facility is in central India. It has three independent units engaged in the production of cephalopsorins, semi-synthetic penicillin and non-beta-lactum products. More than 90% of the products are exported to countries, mainly the United States, Europe, CIS, Africa and the United Kingdom.

Marketing

The company has four regional offices. Each office gets orders from different regions under its control. The order is sent to head office in Delhi and from there, they are distributed to the factories throughout the country. The entire products are produced once the order is confirmed. So in most cases, the company holds minimum finished goods inventory.

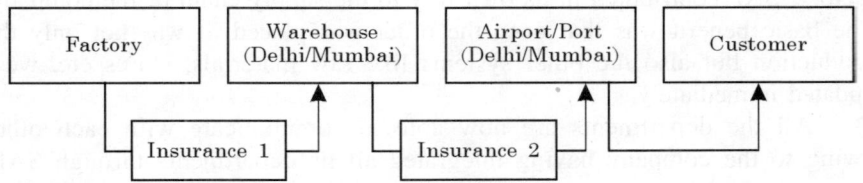

Figure A.1 Supply of finished goods from company to the customer.

Supply Chain (before GSC)

There were no ports and international airports within 100 km of the factory. The products were sent to warehouse in Delhi or Mumbai through refrigerated truck and from there to the respective airport or port. Since the major market for Totman was USA, the customers used to complain about late deliveries. More or less it took 12 days for the delivery to reach the customer abroad, depending upon the distance and mode of transport.

An Inland Container Depot (ICD) was constructed in the year 1998. After this development, the job of delivery by Totman became easy.

Supply Chain (after GSC)

The company got major benefits in terms of cost and manpower due to this development. Moreover, the process helped them reduce the time of delivery to 7 to 8 days instead of 10 to 12 days earlier. The process of supply chain after the introduction of ICD is shown in Figure A.2.

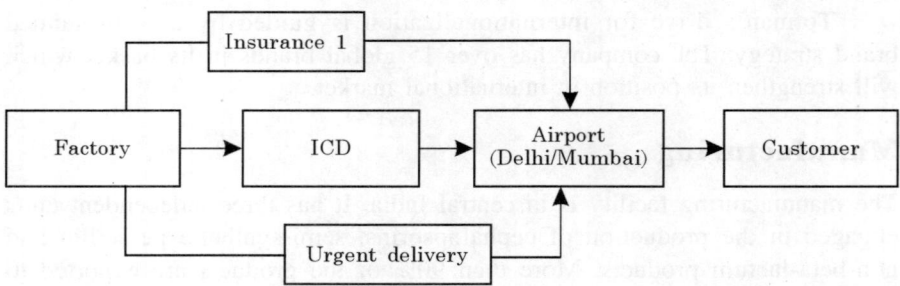

Figure A.2 Supply of finished goods from the company to the customer.

The factory is connected through a dedicated leased line with internet facility. The orders are placed by customers directly to factory. The benefits the company has gained after the introduction of the inland container depot (ICD), are savings in time, direct monitoring by factory, savings in insurance and manpower.

The materials are now cleared by customs in ICD and sent directly to Mumbai or Delhi. In addition, the company has also introduced SAP in the factory. SAP contributed in its own way to the supply chain of the company. The basic benefit was that once the order was placed, it was not only the production but also the other systems like raw materials, stores etc. were updated immediately.

All the departments are now able to communicate with each other owing to the company having integrated all its departments through SAP, except the human resource department. If any customer places an order from abroad or domestically, the company is able to check its stock in all units at a time through SAP. If the material is not available in one unit where the order is placed, that unit can check and find out the availability in other units. Then it communicates to that particular unit so that the stock can be sent to the customer.

Raw Material Supply

The company's inbound logistics organize the supply of raw material from the supplier to the plant. There the material is first tested and then it is sent to the respective production blocks. The company has got its own manufacturing plant for API products. But for making some special medicines, it imports the raw materials. It has got some local suppliers who supply the active pharmacy ingredients for some medicines.

Mr. Manish has established the GSC system and feels it is a competitive advantage for the company. The impact of globalization is constantly taking place in India and he is not comfortable with the present situation. He may soon announce another meeting date to discuss the present situation created by the GSC system. You may play the advisory role of the consultant and give your suggestions to further improve the GSC system.

Case V
CLOSE DOWN OR NOT TO CLOSE DOWN

Surya & Co. is a small-scale tyre manufacturing company. They manufacture tyres for bicycles. The company also supplies tyres directly to the cycle manufacturing company. The company receives some tax reliefs from the state government as a SSI unit.

The company has been facing some problems due to labour unrest. The cost of raw materials has increased substantially along with the labour cost. But competition does not allow the company to increase the cost of the product.

The condensed balance sheet and the income statement are given herewith for the years ended 31 March 2008 and 31 March 2009. In addition, some ratios are also calculated.

The Director of the company likes to recruit one consultant to revive the company. You may play the advisory role of the consultant and give suggestions to improve the profit-earning capacity of the company.

SURYA & CO.
Condensed Balance Sheet for the Years Ended
March 31, 2008 and March 31, 2009

	2009	2008	Increase or Decrease Rs.	%	Percentage of Total Assets 2009	2008
Assets						
Current assets	2,00,500.00	1,59,000.00	41,500.00	26.10	40.06	34.57
Plant and equipment (net)	2,65,000.00	2,43,500.00	21,500.00	8.83	52.95	52.93
Other assets	35,000.00	57,500.00	−22,500.00	−39.13	6.99	12.50
Total	5,00,500.00	4,60,000.00	40,500.00	−8.80	100.00	100.00
Liabilities and Capital						
Liabilities:						
Current liabilities	61,000.00	52,000.00	9,000.00	17.31	12.08	11.30
12% Debentures	1,05,000.00	1,30,000.00	−25,000.00	−19.23	20.79	28.27
Total	1,66,000.00	1,82,000.00	−16,000.00	−8.79	32.87	39.57
Shareholders' equity						
9% preference shares (Rs. 100 each)	55,000.00	55,000.00	0.00		10.89	11.96
Equity shares (Rs. 10 each)	1,30,000.00	1,05,000.00	25,000.00	23.8	25.74	22.83
Premium on issue of shares	40,000.00	25,000.00	15,000.00	60.0	7.92	5.43
Retained earnings	1,14,000.00	93,000.00	21,000.00	22.6	22.57	20.22
Total shareholders equity	3,39,000.00	2,78,000.00	61,000.00	21.9	67.13	60.43
Total	5,05,000.00	4,60,000.00	45,000.00	9.8	100.00	100.00

Continued

SURYA & CO.
Income Statement for the Years Ended March 31, 2008 and March 31, 2009

	2009	2008	Increase or Decrease Rs.	%	Percentage of Total Assets 2009	2008
Net sales	4,55,000	3,80,000	75,000	19.74	100	100
Cost of goods sold	2,70,000	2,15,000	55,000	25.58	59.34	56.58
Gross profit on sales	1,85,000	1,65,000	20,000	12.12	40.66	43.42
Operating expenses						
Selling	63,500	42,500	21,000	49.41	13.96	11.18
Administration	68,000	52,500	15,500	29.52	14.95	13.82
Total	1,31,500	95,000	36,500	38.42	28.90	25.00
Operating income	53,500	70,000	−16,500	−23.57	11.76	18.42
Interest expenses	17,000	20,000	3,000	15.00	3.74	5.26
Income before income taxes	36,500	50,000	−13,500	−27.00	8.02	13.16
Income taxes	19,000	25,000	6,000	24.00	4.18	6.58
Net income	17,500	25,000	−7,500	−30.00	3.85	6.58

Glossary

Application software. Application software is written for or by the users to perform a specific task.

Bit. A binary digit is called a bit. A bit represents either a zero (0) or a one (1).

Byte. A string of eight bits is called byte.

Bandwidth. The capacity of a medium to carry information is called its bandwidth.

Computer crime. Computer crime can be defined as the commission of illegal acts through the use of a computer.

Database Management System (DBMS). A database management system is a collection of programs that enables the organization to store, manipulate and manage its functions effectively.

Data Flow Diagram (DFD). A data flow diagram is a graphical documentation of a system. It describes the system, outlining its features, and interactions with other elements.

Data mining. Data mining is a process of extraction of previously unknown, comprehensible, valid and actionable information from a large database and using the same to make business decisions and support their implementation.

Electronic commerce. Electronic commerce is a concept that describes the process of buying, selling and exchanging products, services and information through internet.

Explicit knowledge. Explicit knowledge is in the form of procedures, methodologies, business rules, case histories, observation reports, forecasts, predictions, design models, articles, products, services, etc.

Field. A group of words or a complete number is called a field.

Hardware. Hardware is the physical equipment used for input, processing and output functions in an information system.

Information system. A set of interrelated components that collects, stores, processes and helps to analyse and support decision-making and control in an organization.

Interorganizational networks. Networks that connect multiple organizations, such as internet are known as interorganizational networks.

Knowledge. Knowledge is a fluid of framed experience, values and contextual information that provides the environment and framework for evaluating and incorporating new experiences and information.

Language. All kinds of software running in the computer system, written in a form that is understandable to the computer, is known as language.

Market research. Market research collects information about consumers, products, marketing methods and marketers.

Microprocessor. Microprocessor is a very large-scale integrated circuit with millions of transistors on a single chip. It integrates the computer's memory, logic and control on a single chip.

Modem. The device used to convert the digital signal into an analog signal and conversely from analog signal to a digital signal, is called a modulator demodulator or modem.

Operating System (OS). The system software which coordinates the various parts of the computer, its peripherals and application software, is known as Operating System (OS).

Organization. An organization is a social entity with structured, directed goal activities that are linked with the external environment.

Packages. Packages are pre-written software for direct use with computers.

Record. A group of related fields makes up a record.

Software. Software consists of detailed instructions or programs that co-ordinate and control hardware components in the information system.

Supply Chain Management (SCM). Managing the whole process of distribution of a product can be defined as Supply Chain Management (SCM).

System. A system is a set of components that interact to accomplish some purpose.

System administrator. The person responsible for installing and maintaining a Local Area Network (LAN) is known as the system administrator.

System analysis. The process of gathering and interpreting facts, diagnosing problems and using the information to recommend improvements to the system is called system analysis.

System design. System design is the process of planning a new business system to replace or complement an existing system.

System software. A set of generalized programs that manage the resources of the computer, such as the Central Processing Unit (CPU), and communicate with other peripherals and devices is known as system software.

Tacit knowledge. Tacit knowledge is composed of insights, perceptions, views, intuitions, hunches, observations, feelings, ideas, mental models, experiences, skills, reasoning and judgment.

References

Chopra, Sunil and Peter Meindl, *Supply Chain Management: Strategy, Planning and Operation,* Prentice-Hall Inc., 2001.

Christopher, Martin, *Logistics and Supply Chain Management: Strategies for Reducing Cost and Improving Service,* Financial Times/Pitman Publishing, 1998.

Currie, Wendy and Bob Galliers (Eds.), *Rethinking Management Information System,* Oxford, 1999.

David and Olsan, *Management Information Systems, Conceptual, Foundations, Structure and Development,* McGraw-Hill Book Company, 1984.

Foss, Bryan and Merlin Stone, *Successful Customer Relationship Marketing,* Cogan Page, U.K. 2001.

Gentle, Michael, *The CRM Project Handbook,* Kogan Page, 2002.

Krishnamurthy, Sandeep, *E-Commerce Management: Text and Cases,* Thomson Learning, 2003.

Laudon, Kenneth C. and Jane Price Laudon, *Management Information Systems: Organisation and Technology,* Macmillan Publishing Co., 1994.

Lee, Efraim Turban Jae, Davod King, and H. Michael Chung, *Electronic Commerce and Managerial Perspective,* Pearson Education Inc., 2000.

Mohamed, H. Peeru and A. Sagadevan, *Customer Relationship Management: A Step-by-Step Approach,* Vikas Publishing, 2002

Oz, Effy, *Management Information Systems,* Thomson Learning, 2000.

Pressman, Roger S., *Software Engineering (A Practitioner's Approach),* 4th ed., McGraw-Hill International Editions (Software Engineering Series), 1997.

Senn, James A., *Analysis and Design of Information Systems,* McGraw-Hill Book Co., Singapore, 1989.

Shelly, Garry B., Thomas J. Cashman and A. Judy Serwatka, *Business Data Communications,* Thomson Learning, 2000.

Singhal, Arvind and Evereh M. Rogers, *India's Communication Revolution, from Bullock Carts to Cyber Marts,* Sage Publication India Pvt. Ltd., 2001.

South, Richard L. Daft, *Organisation Theory and Design,* Sowth Western College Publishing, 2001.

Tanenbaum, Andrew S., *Computer Networks*, 3rd ed., Prentice-Hall of India, 1999.

The Economist Intelligence Unit, Written in Cooperation with Arthur Anderson, *Managing Business Risks in the Information Age,* Universities Press, 2000.

The Economist of Newspaper Ltd., *E-Trends,* 2001.

Umbaugh, Robert E. (Ed.), *Handbook of IS Management,* Viva Books Private Limited, 1999.

Index

American National Standard Institute (ANSI), 22
American Standard Code for Information Interchange (ASCII), 22
Arithmetic Logic Unit (ALU), 23
Artificial intelligence, 38, 154
Auction, 109, 172
Automated Teller Machine (ATM), 40, 56, 68

Bandwidth, 57, 62
Bar code, 9, 28
Basic Input Output System (BIOS), 24
Benchmark, 136, 170
Binary digit, 21
BPR, 74
Brainstorming, 136
Brand, 111, 135
Brick-and-click, 108
Brick-and-mortar, 131, 153
Business reengineering, 6
Business-to-business (B2B), 109, 118, 127
Business-to-consumer (B2C), 108, 118
Business-to-government (B2G), 109

Cable
    coaxial, 58
    fibre optic, 59
    twisted, 57
Cache memory, 24
Call centres, 6, 83, 92, 157
Card reader, 54
Cartridge, 25, 30
Cash book, 3
Cathode Ray Tube (CRT), 28
CD-ROM, 25

Cellular, 57, 60, 61
Central Processing Unit (CPU), 21
Chief Executive Officer (CEO), 14, 91, 160, 182
Chip, 22, 24, 134
Client/server, 56, 148
CMYK, 30
Commission, 111, 175
Competitive advantage, 1, 121, 191
Compiler, 38
Computer Aided Design (CAD), 39, 41
Computer Aided Manufacturing (CAM), 39
Computer crime, 175
Constant Angular Velocity (CAV), 26
Constant Linear Velocity (CLV), 26
Consumer-to-consumer (C2C), 109
Control
    mechanism, 3
    unit, 22, 23
Control Panel, 24, 36, 41, 92,
Customer Interaction Centres (CICs), 131
Customer Relationship Management (CRM), 81, 90, 129–141
Customization, 85, 112, 130, 184

Data
    analysis, 11, 53, 117, 139
    collection, 117, 131
    dictionary, 46, 47, 102
    external, 2, 144, 146
    flow, 57, 99, 100
    internal, 2, 144, 146
    mining, 53, 138–140
    store, 99, 100
    warehouse, 53, 143, 144, 161
    worker, 6, 14, 16

Data Definition Language (DDL), 46, 47
Data Flow Diagram (DFD), 99, 102
Data Manipulation Language (DML), 46, 47
Database
    administration, 51
    management, 43–54, 144
Database model
    hierarchical, 47
    network, 49
    relational, 49
Decision Support System (DSS), 15, 17, 142–155
Demographics, 111
Digital
    camera, 28
    files, 16, 28
Digital Audio Tape (DAT), 25
Disk
    compact, 25
    floppy, 7, 25
    hard, 7, 25, 63
    optical, 25
Disk Operating System (DOS), 35, 67
Distributed processing, 89
Dot matrix, 29, 30
Downstream, 123, 124
Drill-down, 147, 153, 161

EBCDIC, 22
E-business, 136, 170–172
Electronic commerce, 72, 107–110
E-mail, 7, 175
Empowered, 90, 92, 136
End-user, 39, 101
Enterprise Resource Planning (ERP), 19, 40, 124, 184
Ethics, 174, 178
Executive Information System (EIS), 15, 143, 157–163
Executive Support System (ESS), 17, 143, 162
Expert systems, 38, 154, 155
External entity, 99, 100

Feasibility
    economic, 98
    operational, 98
    technical, 98
Feedback system, 3
Field, 43
File, 43
Frequency, 59, 61

Geographic Information System (GIS), 143, 146, 147
Geosynchronous Earth Orbiting Satellites (GEOSs), 60
Graphical User Interface (GUI), 35, 36
Group Decision Support System (GDSS), 143

Hardware, 7, 21–32, 65, 178

Information
    architecture, 6, 89
    system, 1, 2
    technology, 1, 2, 5
Intellectual property, 176, 177
Intermediaries, 112, 119
Intermediation, 113
Interorganizational system, 53
Interpreter, 35, 38
Intranet, 125, 126
ISDN, 107

Key Performance Indicator (KPI), 153
Knowledge
    explicit, 165
    management, 165–172
    organisation, 165, 166, 172
    tacit, 165, 166, 172
    usage, 170
    worker, 165–172

Language
    assembly, 37
    high-level, 38
    machine, 37, 38
    programming, 37–39
Learning organisation, 166
Local Area Network (LAN), 56, 65
Logical operation, 23
Logistics, 77, 122
    inbound, 122, 189
    outbound, 122, 187
Low Earth Orbiting Satellites (LEOSs), 60, 61

Magnetic
    disk, 25
    tape, 25, 45
Magnetic Ink Character Recognition (MICR), 27

Mailing list, 34
Mainframe, 26, 48, 62, 161
Make-buy, 105
Management Information Systems (MIS), 11–19
Market research, 117, 118, 136
Matchmaking, 116, 172
Medical transcription, 6, 78, 90
Medium
    conducted, 57
    radiated, 57
Medium Earth Orbiting Satellites (MEOSs), 61
Memory
    primary, 24
    secondary, 24
Methodologies, 96, 138, 165
Microcomputer, 25–27, 35
Microprocessor, 22
Microwave, 57, 59, 60, 63
Modem, 29, 65
Monochrome Display Adaptor (MDA), 28–29
Multi
    media, 27, 29, 40
    processing, 34, 35
    programming, 34, 35
    tasking, 35
    user, 30, 146, 147

Network
    cards, 31, 67
    management, 36, 68, 69

Object Oriented Programming (OOP), 38, 104
Online Analytical Processing (OLAP), 53, 131, 143, 146
Optical Character Recognition (OCR), 27
Organization culture, 87
Outsourcing, 77–87
Office automation, 15, 39–41, 81

Package, 38
Parallel port, 21, 30
Patent, 176
Peripherals, 27, 34, 65
Phase
    analysis, 97, 99
    construction, 97, 101
    design, 97, 100
    implementation, 97, 101

    initiation/initial survey, 97
    maintenance, 97, 101
Pilot project, 119
Plotter, 28, 31
Point of purchase, 9
Primary storage, 24, 35
Printer
    impact, 29
    non-impact, 29, 31
Private network, 65
Process, 2, 13
Processor, 7, 21, 28
Production, 6, 7
Program, 5, 35
Programmer, 33, 37, 105
Programming, 33
Prototype, 18, 97, 102
Psychographic, 111
Public network, 65

Random Access Memory (RAM), 24, 25, 83
Record, 43
Register, 24, 73
Reintermediation, 113
Relational Database Management System (RDBMS), 47
Repetitive Stress Injury (RSI), 178
Resolution, 29
Retailer, 127
Retailing, 110, 111
ROM
    Erasable Programmable Read Only Memory (EPROM), 24
    Programmable Read Only Memcry (PROM), 24

Sales Force Automation (SFA), 126
Sales register, 3
Satellite, 57, 60, 67
Scanner, 9, 28
Segment, 40, 48
Segmentation, 133, 136
Serial port, 21, 27
Service sectors, 133
Shielded Twisted Pair (STP), 57
Simulation, 89, 151
Software
    application, 34
    customized, 40
    embedded, 40
    readymade, 40
    system, 34

Standard Operating Procedure (SOP), 70, 87, 163, 176
Storage unit, 7, 23
   primary, 23
   secondary, 23
Stores, 123
Structured Query Language (SQL), 38, 47
Supercomputer, 26
Supplier, 127
Supplier Management System (SMS), 126
Supply Chain Management (SCM), 90, 121–128, 188
Supply chain, 6, 189
SVGA, 28
System
   analysis, 94
   design, 94
System Development Life Cycle Method (SDLC), 97

Telecommunication, 7, 9, 56, 79
Thin Flim Transistor (TFT), 31
Time sharing, 34
Token ring, 64
Topology
   bus, 63, 64
   ring, 63, 64
   star, 62, 64

Total Quality Management (TQM), 6
Transmission
   duplex, 57
   simplex, 57

Upstream, 118, 123
Unique Selling Proposition (USP), 6
Universal Serial Bus (USB), 21, 30
Unshielded Twisted Pair (UTP), 57, 61

Value
   engineering, 125, 136
   proportion, 134, 169
Very Small Apparatus Terminals (VSATs), 60
Video Graphics Array (VGA), 28, 29
Virtual storage, 35
Visual Display Unit (VDU), 28

Wide Area Network (WAN), 62, 65, 67
Word processing, 9, 16
Work
   culture, 9, 89, 163
   station, 26, 147
World Wide Web (WWW), 130, 143

Zero pricing, 118